FRANCE

an amazingly short history

by
BOB FOWKE

Travelbrief Publications

Published in 2004 by Travelbrief Publications

0-9548351-1-5

10 9 8 7 6 5 4 3 2 1

Travelbrief Publications
7 Brougham Square, Shrewsbury SY3 7PE

Printed and bound by Cambrian Printers, UK

CONTENTS

Acknowledgement
With thanks to Andrew Mee and Robert Branton. Their help with the writing of this book has been invaluable.

INTRODUCTION
AN APOLOGY OF SORTS

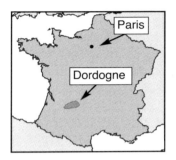

Bonjour!

The Dordogne in south-west France is very beautiful, a land of limestone hills, of dawdling rivers and impossibly pretty towns. It's well worth a visit, even if it's a long drive from Paris and even if nowadays it's been rather bought up by second-homers from Britain and other countries. Apart from being beautiful, the Dordogne contains some of the most fascinating prehistoric sites in France, including the cave paintings of Lascaux (from around 15,000 BC), accidentally discovered by a puppy called Robot in 1940.

Robot was out for an afternoon walk with his owner, a boy called Simon, and a group of Simon's friends when he discovered the cave of Lascaux. He disappeared while the boys were looking in another direction. It must have been a dreadful shock - a sudden fall down a hole in the ground and there he was, plunged back 17,000 years, completely without warning.

France has a very long and very full history. To attempt to sum it up in a mere 128 pages is probably an act of insanity. It's not just the length of France's history which is troubling, it's the sheer, mind-boggling importance of the place. France has been right at the centre of European culture for more than a thousand years. Indeed, to some extent, the history of France *is* the history of Europe.

But on the other hand - history is as much about leaving things out as putting things in. Without leaving things out, history books would be impossible. Seen from this point of view, a 128-page history of France is fine.

All of which is by way of apologising for all the steamy love affairs, bloody battles, great artists, gorgeous women, handsome men, brilliant scientists, saints, misfits, mad fools and megalomaniacs which France has produced in glorious abundance over the centuries but which this history single-mindedly ignores. Those that are left in will just have to stand for all the others who've been left out. Sorry.

Bob Fowke, July 2004

If you're in the Dordogne

About eighty kilometres south of Limoges, the Vézère Valley runs northeast from the confluence of the Vézère and the Dordogne rivers. The valley contains spectacular remains of early man. In addition to the caves of Lascaux, there are further hundreds of prehistoric paintings at the *Grotte* (Cave) *de Font de Gaume*, and the *Grotte de Rouffignac*. Since their discovery in 1940, the paintings of Lascaux have been damaged by the breath of too many tourists so they're now closed to the public. They've been recreated at Lascaux II nearby.

FRANCE BEFORE WINE

THE GRIM TRUTH

Big teeth and other things

As far back as 90,000 BC, which is an amazingly long time ago, people were already living in the area of what is now France. There weren't very many of them by modern standards - thousands rather than millions - but they stuck it out through all that the prehistoric world could throw at them: ice ages, sabre-toothed tigers, giant elk, a complete absence of wine. They were strong and stocky these early people, with big brow ridges, big teeth and large powerful hands. Their brains were as large or larger than the brains of modern humans. They're known as Neanderthalers* and although their way of life was rather basic, they already used fire to cook. Charred bones left at their settlements are evidence that 'cuisine' in what is now France has an extremely long history, considerably longer than the word 'French' - and that initially it included mastodon.

Around 37,000 BC the Neanderthalers were replaced by a new race of humans, the Cro-Magnons. Cro-Magnons were taller than Neanderthalers and were probably more attractive to modern eyes, having smaller brow ridges and daintier hands. In fact, physically, they were modern humans. They were also very wonderful artists. It was

*From the Neander valley in southern Germany where remains were discovered, back in 1856.

the Cro-Magnons who created the beautiful cave paintings at Lascaux discovered by Robot in 1940 (see introduction).

Dragons' teeth

Neanderthalers and Cro-Magnons went the way of all flesh. Thousands of years passed. For countless centuries, anonymous tribes wandered the forests forming and reforming in a million petty skirmishes, alliances, feuds, marriages and other dramas, for reasons once crucially important but now lost for ever in the mists of time.

Then around 7,000 BC, farming began. The first small clearings were hacked from the wilderness. A remarkable culture developed. Just outside the village of Carnac in Brittany there's an immense system of standing stones. They're laid out in long parallel lines like rows of dragons' teeth, heading roughly north-east from the village. They're not as big as the stones of Stonehenge, but there's a lot more of them - around three thousand in all. Work on these stones began before 5,000 BC - long before the building of the pyramids. Unfortunately we have no definite idea what forgotten beliefs led the stone builders to create these extraordinary monuments.

> **If you're in Brittany**
> Carnac Ville is an attractive village on the coast of the Baie de Quiberon, about 30 kilometres west of Vannes. As well as long lines of menhirs (individual standing stones), there are dolmens (two stones with another across the top) and tumuli (earth mounds over dolmens). The whole of the Morbihan area is littered with Neolithic remains.

Big thugs

Several thousand more years passed. The stone builders built their monuments and lived in their villages. They began to work bronze and their culture became quite sophisticated.

Then, from around 1,200 BC, things changed yet again. Not for the last time in the history of the region, the natives were invaded by large, fair-haired northerners. The newcomers of 1,200 BC used to bleach their already fair hair and often wore it in spikes when going into battle. They may also have dyed their skin blue with woad. They're known as the 'Celts' and they were a grim lot. It's said that in the early days they cut the tongues from captured womenfolk to ensure that any children would grow up speaking Celtic. This may be part of the reason why no one knows what language was spoken during the stone-building culture which went before them.

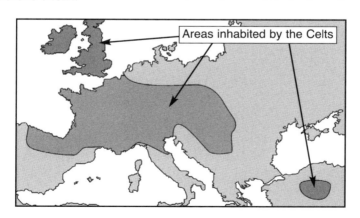

Areas inhabited by the Celts

The Celts were extremely aggressive. They displaced or combined with the local inhabitants and then proceeded to raid far and wide across Europe, capturing and burning Rome itself, apart from its fortress, in 390 BC.

With the coming of the Celts, the history of what is now France, the kind that's written down, really began. But, despite the tongue cutting, it wasn't written down in Celtic. The Celts couldn't write. It was written down by the Greeks and, more importantly, by the Romans, who feared the Celts and had good reason to write about them. It's to the Greeks and Romans that we owe our first descriptions of France, then called 'Gaul' after the Latin name for its inhabitants.

French History
(and prehistory)

1945 - AD	Up to now
1917-1945 AD	Two World Wars plus interwar years
1800 -	Nineteenth century
1789-1815 AD	French Revolution and Napoleonic Wars
1700 -	Eighteenth century
1643-1715 AD	Louis XIV
1562-1590s	Wars of Religion
1337-1453 AD	Hundred Years' War - Joan of Arc
447-989 AD	Early Middle Ages - Carolingians and Merovingians
BC 52 - 486 AD	Romans
c. BC 1,200 -	Celts
c. BC 5,000 -	Early stuff - Carnac
BC 90,000 -	Really early stuff - Neanderthalers and Cro-Magnons

MEN WITH MOUSTACHES
CELTS HAD THEM, ROMANS DIDN'T

In Brief - Gaul	
BC 1,200-500	Coming of the Celts.
c. BC 600	Marseille founded by the Greeks.
BC 121	Provence founded by the Romans.
BC 58-50	Roman conquest of Gaul.
BC 52	Revolt of Vercingetorix.

A hilltop in Central Gaul (modern France)

It was September 52 BC. Julius Caesar, smooth-shaven Roman general and politician, was sitting on a campaign chair outside the recently conquered fortress of Alesia. He was slightly nervous. Around him, on a large, prancing warhorse and dressed in the full battle armour of a barbarian chieftain, circled Vercingetorix, war leader of the ancient Gauls. Vercingetorix was tall and tough with long, fair hair and a drooping moustache. Suddenly, he stopped circling and leaped from his horse. He tore off its rich harness set with silver, coral and gold and threw it at Caesar's feet. Then he took off his own armour and threw that at Caesar's feet as well. Then he sat down on the ground to await his fate.

If you're near Dijon

Alesia is the modern village of Alise-Sainte-Reine, which is about twenty miles north-west of Dijon as the crow flies. There's a museum close by the village and a statue of Vercingetorix on a nearby hill.

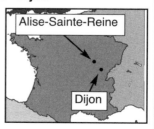

Caesar's victory outside the fortress of Alesia in 52 BC was the last act in Rome's conquest of Gaul. When Alesia fell, Vercingetorix's rebellion, the last and greatest Gallic (from the Latin 'Gallus', a Gaul) uprising against Roman rule, was finally over. By surrendering and not running away as he could have done, Vercingetorix hoped to save his people from Roman reprisals. His surrender was a magnificent gesture, typical of the ancient Gauls, but it was no use to him personally. He was sent in chains to Rome where, six years later, he was paraded through the streets behind Caesar's chariot before being strangled.

Drumsticks at dawn
Despite all the modern talk of a 'Celtic Fringe', the Gauls were originally central Europeans, close relatives of the ancient Germans. This was why they tended to be tall and fair-haired with fair skin like Vercingetorix. It was also why they frightened the Romans who were shorter, if better organised.

Like the ancient Germans, the Gauls were much given to drunkenness and overeating. They loved rich cloths and gold ornaments. According to one Roman observer, their chief characteristics were 'irritability and a mad love of war'. At their frequent banquets, the drumsticks of chickens went to guests of honour - fights to the death over who should eat the drumstick were not unknown. They often rushed into battle stark naked to show how brave they were. With little in the way of tactics, they could still fight like devils, as was proved by Vercingetorix.

The sacred symbol of the Gauls was the wild boar, known for its ferocious temper. Their pigs, which wandered free in the fields, were said to be as fierce as wolves.

The Romans admired the size and bravery of the Gauls but despised them because they were barbarians. Barbarian, of course, is a relative word. These ancient ancestors of the French built no great stone monuments like the stone builders had done, or stone cities like the civilisations of the south, and they had no written language, but at least they were clean - cleaner than the Romans despite the Roman love of baths. The Celts invented soap. They also developed the working of iron, enamelling, vegetable dyes, a mechanical reaper and a plough, and they did have cities of sorts, if not recognisable as such by the Romans.

Romans

The Roman conquest of Gaul started back in 121 BC with the formation of the 'Province' (modern Provence) around the city of Marseille, which had been founded as a trading colony by ancient Greeks in 600 BC. The Province stretched from Marseille as far north as Lake Geneva.

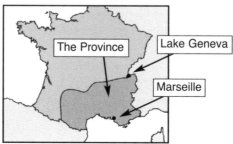

The Province / Lake Geneva / Marseille

By the time of Vercingetorix's uprising, Provence was already Romanised. It had cities and spacious public buildings and the language of the rulers was Latin, as spoken by the Romans. Now that Vercingetorix was out of the way, the rest of Gaul followed suit. Large numbers of retired Roman soldiers were given land to settle on, and Gauls and Romans soon fused to create a blend of cultures known as Gallo-Roman. Meanwhile Gaul grew fat. Celtic traders made use of new, well-made Roman roads. Large villas sprang up in the countryside. The wine industry got going. Within a century, Latin took over from Celtic as the main language, although Celtic continued to be spoken in more rural areas.

If you're in the south
Nîmes, *Colonia Nemausensis* in Roman times, contains the most impressive Roman remains in France: a magnificent amphitheatre for gladiator fights and an incredibly well-preserved temple, the *Maison Carrée*. Twenty-three kilometres north of Nîmes the massive, Roman Pont du Gard bridge and aqueduct once carried water to the town.

Wine as a commercial product was first introduced into Gaul by the Romans. There were two varieties in Roman Gaul: the biturica *which grew in the region of modern Bordeaux and was better known for quantity than quality and the* piccata *which grew along the Rhône valley. Wine soon became a major export from the region, as it has been ever since.*

Paris
Under Roman rule, the old, Gallic tribal centres remained as the central cities of their regions. Augusta Trèves for

instance was the city of the tribe of the Trevirii, and Paris on its island on the River Seine, then called Lutetia Parisiorum, was the city of the Parisii, which probably meant 'boat people'. These Gallo-Roman cities boasted Roman amenities such as baths and temples.

> **If you're in Paris**
> The site of the original settlement of the Parisii and then of Lutetia Parisiorum was the Ile de la Cité in the middle of the River Seine, the heart of historic Paris. The Cathedral of Notre Dame (dating from 1163 but replacing an earlier cathedral) stands on the site of a Roman temple to the god Jupiter.

For many years, Lyon was the chief city of Roman Gaul but, in the fourth century AD, Paris took over. Paris was on the Seine and it was also at the hub of a network of roads, built to cope with the expanding economy of Roman Gaul. At the height of the Roman Empire, the main road from Paris to Orléans was so busy that a parallel relief road, the *Via Inferior* was built to take the excess traffic. The name survives in garbled form in the Parisian Avenue 'Renfert-Rocher'.

Headless bishops
Legend has it that Saint Denis, Bishop of Paris, along with two companions, was beheaded in Paris in AD 258 after being subjected to various horrible tortures by the Roman authorities. The execution took place on Mons Martyrum (Martyrs' Mount = modern Montmartre). This was during a persecution of Christians in the reign of the Roman Emperor Valerian. According to legend, Denis is said to have picked up his decapitated head, washed it

and carried it several kilometres to what is now the suburb of Saint Denis. The Abbey of St. Denis stands where he's buried.

> **If you're in Paris**
> Originally a simple shrine, the Abbey of St. Denis was founded by King Dagobert (reigned 628-637). It was largely rebuilt under Abbot Suger (1081-1155) and is the first major Gothic-style building in the world.

Christianity arrived in Gaul via the old Greek colony of Marseille in about AD 63, a mere thirty years after the crucifixion of Christ. Many citizens of Marseille still spoke Greek even at that late date and were therefore able to understand the Christian message - Greek was the language of the eastern Mediterranean and the language in which Christianity was first preached to non-Jews. From Marseille, the new religion spread northward and after a while most large cities contained a small Christian community. A letter from the Christians of Lyon to Christians in Asia, written in AD 181, describes a typical community: a lawyer, an upper-class woman, some slaves and other lowly citizens and a ninety-year-old bishop called Pothinus.

Bishops were very important. They were the leaders and, like Denis, in times of persecution they paid the price. Ironically, when the Roman Empire fell to pieces in the dark and dangerous fifth century, those pieces were picked up by none other than those same bishops, previously so terribly persecuted. It was the Christian Church which kept alive the remains of Roman civilisation after the Roman Empire had fallen. Before that time of course, Christianity had become the official religion of the Empire and bishops had become powerful members of the establishment.

Germans

The problem for France (and before that for Gaul) has always been its north-east frontier. In the east and south-east there's the Alps, in the south there's the Mediterranean Sea, in the south-west there's the Pyrenees and in the west there's the Atlantic, the

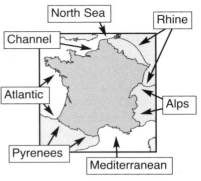

Channel and the North Sea - but in the north-east there's nothing apart from the River Rhine, which has never been much of a barrier. And beyond the Rhine there's always been the Germans. In Roman times they were a pretty savage bunch. To keep the Germans at bay, the Romans maintained a huge army of up to 200,000 soldiers strung out on both sides of the river in a system of military camps and other fortifications.

If you're in Strasbourg

Strasbourg, the main city of Alsace, started life as the Roman military camp, *Argentoratum*, one of over fifty such camps built along the River Rhine between BC 16 and BC 12 by the Roman general Drusus, brother of the Emperor Tiberius. (The camp later joined up with the local village *Strateburgum*, whence the name Strasbourg.) The Cathedral is built on the site of a Roman temple which once overlooked the camp. Some Roman remains are on display in the *Musée Archéologique* in the basement of the Château de Rohan near the cathedral.

For more than two hundred years the legions kept the Germans at bay, but German pressure on the frontier grew ever stronger. In 275-76 tribes of Alemanni, Franks and Burgundes fought their way south across Gaul, burning and pillaging as they went. The tribesmen were joined by large numbers of escaped slaves who were only too happy to attack their former owners. Gallo-Roman society almost collapsed.

The Germans of 275-76 were driven out but nothing was the same after that. From now on towns began to be fortified with strong walls, and, more importantly, the Romans began to rely on 'tame' Germans to keep the other Germans out. The tame Germans, including Franks and Burgundes, were granted land for their families as had been the custom for retired Roman soldiers in years gone by, although, unlike the Romans, the tame Germans were looked down on. Marriage between Gauls and Germans was forbidden, as it was between freemen and slaves.

Time went by and the Empire weakened still further. For safety, the Gauls retreated into their old tribal units. Towns dropped their Latin names: Augusta Treves became Trèves and Lutetia Parisiorum became Paris. Then, in the fifth century, German tribes attacked in force, driven to it by meaner, nastier barbarians from the east under the leadership of Attila the Hun, 'Scourge of God'. This time there was no recovery and no time to regroup. German attacks continued and grew fiercer and fiercer. By AD 500, the Roman Empire was a tattered wreck and the map of Gaul and southern Germany had been completely redrawn. In the east there was an independent kingdom called Burgundy founded by the

German Burgundes, in the south a kingdom of the equally German Visigoths.

And in the north-east, there was a kingdom of the Franks.

TO BE FRANK
AND RATHER BRUTAL

In brief - the early Middle Ages	
481 AD	Start of first Frankish kingdom under Clovis.
751-989	Merovingian dynasty.
768-814	Carolingian dynasty.
885-86	Reign of Charlemagne.
911	Founding of Normandy by Rollo.

Toughs with topknots

'Frank' comes from an old German word *'franca'* meaning 'brave'. It's where the word 'France' comes from. The Franks invaded from what is now Belgium. They had a smattering of Roman culture from having lived so long in the border regions, but they were still barbarians. Frankish warriors fought on foot and wielded a double-headed axe as their weapon of choice. They wore their hair in topknots with the back of the head shaved, except for their kings who wore it long at the back.

The sacred symbol of the Franks was the bee. They were fond of honey both as a sweetener and when fermented into mead. It's thought that the bee symbol may have evolved into the *Fleur de Lis* on the French royal coat of arms.

By medieval times, knowledge of the French monarchy's German origins had been all but lost. Interestingly, in 1714, a French scholar called Nicolas Feret was imprisoned in the Bastille for demonstrating that the Franks were really Germans.

Clovis and the Catholics

Clovis (ruled 481-511), who led the initial invasion of the Franks, was a thoroughly nasty piece of work. In his ferocious pursuit of power he killed at least ten kings or the sons of kings, including several close relatives, some of them only children, either by his own hand or by arrangement with others. Not content with carving out a kingdom from the lands controlled by the remains of the Romans, by 509 he had brutally crushed the rival Visigoth and Burgundian kingdoms and made himself master not only of Gaul but also of a large chunk of what are now Belgium and southern Germany. As it ended up, Clovis's kingdom was larger than modern France, but he's still seen as the first king of 'France'.

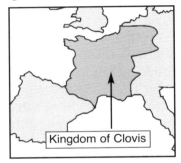

Kingdom of Clovis

On 1 January 509, Clovis was appointed 'Patrician' of all the Roman Empire to the west of the Alps in a solemn ceremony at Tours. A Patrician was a sort of deputy for the Roman Emperor. Discarding the normal costume of a Frankish king although with his royal long hair still flowing down his back, he wore a white Roman toga with a purple border round the edge and carried an ivory rod in his right hand. The Roman Empire might have collapsed under the weight of barbarian invasion but there was still an emperor of sorts in Italy and another in Constantinople* (modern Istanbul) and the

*Clovis was Patrician to the eastern Emperor (based in Constantinople), not the western one.

Empire was still the legal government. Appointment as Patrician put the seal on Clovis's conquests.

The magnificent ceremony at Tours was led by a huddle of Catholic bishops and clergymen. In the eyes of these priests, Clovis was a good man despite being a murderer and a megalomaniac, or perhaps because of it. This was because he supported and nourished the Catholic faith. God, after all, works in mysterious ways. Back in 493, Clovis had had the good sense to marry Clotilda, a Catholic, Burgundian princess. From that time on Clovis and the Catholics had been allies against the Burgundians and Visigoths who were Arians* (with a few exceptions such as Clotilda), a different type of Christian.

The marriage of Clovis and Clotilda is why France is a Catholic country today.

If you're in Reims

Reims, the main city of the Department of the Marne, in Champagne where the wine comes from, was where French monarchs were traditionally crowned until the Revolution of 1789. This tradition dated back to AD 496 when Clovis was baptised there, at the instigation of Clotilda, along with 3,000 of his warriors. The Church of St. Remi, in the Place St. Remi, is named after Remigius, the bishop who baptised them.

Merovingians

Clovis and his descendants are known as the Merovingians, named after Meroveus, a shadowy ancestor who fought with the Romans against Attila the Hun back in 451. Their dynasty, the Merovingian

*Not to be confused with 'Aryan', a word meaning roughly 'Indo-European' but misused by the Nazis to mean anyone generally blond and north-European.

dynasty, ruled for about a hundred years. They were a bad lot. Less like kings than heavily armed thugs, the Merovingians behaved like gangster bosses squabbling over the family territory rather than kings looking after their subjects. Clotaire I (reigned 558-562), Clovis's youngest son, had six wives in total, some simultaneously, including the widowed mother of two nephews whom he killed when they were still children. He also burned to death a rebellious son and the son's young family by shutting them up in a cottage and setting fire to it.

To be fair, Clotaire I was worse than average. Chilperic I (reigned 566-84), one of Clovis's grandsons, was a poet who tried to reform the writing of popular Latin, then rapidly evolving into French. (Those who rejected his suggestions had their eyes put out.) And Dagobert I (reigned 628-37), Chilperic's grandson, was almost good. He committed relatively few murders and managed to enlarge the kingdom. His reign was the high point of Merovingian rule.

Mayors of the Palace
By 732, the Franks had scarcely changed their way of fighting since the time of the Roman Empire. They still mainly fought on foot.

In 732, central France was invaded by a formidable Arab army under Abd ar-Rahman, the governor of Muslim Spain, then under Arab rule. The Arabs were fired up with Islamic zeal, it being only a hundred years since the death of the prophet Mohammed in 632. The Franks under their young and brilliant leader Charles Martel ('The Hammer') gathered just outside Tours to fight them off. Under Charles's leadership, the Franks stood firm in the battle which followed, only moving to collect their throwing axes and spears after each Arab cavalry charge was over. The last Arab charge took place around sunset. During the night, the Arabs left their camp and all its riches to the Franks and started the long retreat south.

Charles Martel, saviour of Christian Europe, was never king of the Franks as such. Officially he was a 'Mayor of the Palace' or *major domus*, a sort of chief minister to three successive Merovingian kings. But there was no doubt where real power lay. As if to prove the point, when he came of age, Charles defeated one king, Childeric II, and following this, another king, Clotaire IV of Austrasia (the northeast portion of the Frankish domains) only became a king because Charles backed him.

By 732 the Merovingian kings were kings in name only, feeble characters known to history as the *rois fainéants* or 'do-nothing' kings. The only thing still royal about them was their long hair. Their men of business, the Mayors of the Palace, filled the power vacuum. Finally in AD 751, the Merovingians faded out completely. Childeric III, the last Merovingian king, was simply packed off to a monastery by Pepin the Short, son of Charles Martel. Pepin took the crown for himself. The Pope gave his blessing, switching his support from the feeble Childeric III to the dynamic Pepin with the words:

It is better to call him king who wields the power, rather than him who is deprived of it.

Three years later, on 28 July 754, a new Pope was persuaded to anoint Pepin with holy oil in a solemn ceremony in the Abbey of St. Denis outside Paris (built in memory of Denis the Martyr). This was very important. From that day on, the kings of France could claim to be chosen by God - a crucial bargaining chip when dealing with powerful nobles in years to come. French nobles were frequently richer and more powerful than the French king but the holy oil meant that the king was always superior.

Charlemagne
In the late nineteenth century, a group of historians opened a tomb dating from the early ninth century in the Abbey of St. Denis. Inside they found the skeleton of a man who had once stood at least six feet three inches tall in his socks, or rather cross-garters. This was the skeleton of the Emperor Charlemagne (reigned 768-814), son of Pepin the Short.

In life, at a time when the average height of a man wasn't much over five feet, Charlemagne must have seemed an overpowering figure with his long golden hair and his flowing beard. According to contemporaries, the only things about him which weren't overpowering were his high-pitched voice and a tendency to be talkative. Pepin may have been the first non-Merovingian king of France but for good reason the name of the family dynasty 'Carolingian' comes from his jovial, ruthless son Charlemagne.

Frankish domains had included parts of what are now Belgium and southern Germany since 500. Charlemagne extended this to include all German tribes north of the Rhine, ie a large chunk of modern Germany, and also the Lombard kingdom of northern Italy. Europe was never so united again, not until another Frenchman, the

Emperor Napoleon, created a new French Empire a thousand years later. At the summit of his power, on Christmas Day 800, Charlemagne was proclaimed Roman Emperor by Pope Leo III in St. Peter's church in Rome, at the Pope's behest. Higher than this, no one could go.

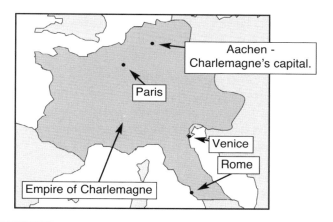

Aachen - Charlemagne's capital.

Paris

Venice

Rome

Empire of Charlemagne

If you're in Aachen

Aachen (Aix-la-Chapelle in French), is in Germany near the German/ Dutch/ Belgian border. For many years, it was Charlemagne's northern capital. The chapel of his palace still stands, and in the gallery you can see his marble throne, used for for centuries afterwards for the coronations of German Emperors. Aachen was once a Roman spa town. Charlemagne chose it because he loved swimming, often inviting friends and guests to join him. According to his courtier Einhard, sometimes up to a hundred men would swim together in the warm waters.

Going French

The basic unit of Charlemagne's empire was the county, ruled over by a count. Viscounts were sometimes appointed to stand in for counts and border counties might be grouped into 'marches' and administered by marquises. To start with, the counts and other officials were appointed, but gradually Charlemagne allowed them to leave their jobs to their sons:

> *Duke - a great leader*
> *Count - official who ran a county*
> *Viscount - a count's deputy*
> *Marquis - guardian of a march or border region*

Once state officials were able to inherit their positions, their job titles became marks of nobility first and job titles second. As a result, sons of rough, tough Frankish warriors started to think of themselves as posh, upper-class nobles.

The new nobility no longer spoke a dialect of German; they spoke French, which emerged gradually from Latin during the period of Frankish rule. The first official document in French dates from around 842, an oath sworn by two of Charlemagne's grandsons. This document is in an early form of the French which evolved in northern France. It was called *langue d'oïl* because speakers said *oui* to mean 'yes'. In the south people spoke *langue d'oc* and said *oc* to mean 'yes'. *Langue d'oïl* evolved into modern standard French but for hundreds of years *langue d'oc* was more respected as a dialect. *Langue d'oïl* speakers would sometimes apologise for their rough speech when addressing southerners.

Normandy and the northmen
In 840, twenty-six years after Charlemagne died, yet another wave of large, fair-haired thugs attacked the land of the Franks. The new lot were even larger and came from Scandinavia, even further north than where the Franks had come from. These new invaders were

Vikings. They worshipped Thor and Odin and went in for human sacrifice.

For over fifty years, the Vikings plundered Frankish lands in a long orgy of destruction. Their work was made easier because, after the death of Charlemagne, the Franks were hopelessly divided. Late Carolingian rulers fought each other as much as they fought the invaders and are notable for a number of less than complimentary nicknames: Louis the Stammerer (ruled 877-79), Charles the Fat (ruled 844-88) and Charles the Simple (ruled 898-922). The Vikings used the river system to raid deep inland, attacking Paris on several occasions. In fact, in 886 they attacked it in force and were only just driven off. By 911, they'd become such a problem that Charles the Simple bought off the then Viking leader by making him Count of Rouen and giving him lands in the region of the city.

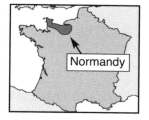

These lands came to be called Normandy, 'land of the Northmen'. The Viking leader who received this gift was Rollo the Ganger - 'Ganger' because he was so huge that he couldn't easily ride a horse and had to 'gang' about on foot. It's said that during the ceremony Rollo refused to bow the knee to Charles. Instead, he lifted Charles's foot to kiss it and sent Charles tumbling backwards. In return for being made a count, Rollo promised to stop his Viking raids on the lands of the French king and became a Christian of sorts, although on his deathbed he ordered human sacrifices as well as gifts to the Church.

THE MIDDLE AGES
WHEN KNIGHTS WERE BOLD

In Brief	
987-1328	The Capetian Dynasty.
*c.*1130	Start of Gothic architecture.
1096	The First Crusade sets off.
1337-1453	Hundred Years' War.
1328-1589	The Valois Dynasty.
c. 1412-1431	Joan of Arc.

A cloak too far

Early medieval France was the richest country in Europe. Paris was more than twice the size and population of London, and the population of France as a whole was a lot more than that of any other European kingdom.

France was rich but it was decentralised and its kings had trouble controlling it. When Louis V 'Do-Nothing', last of the Carolingians, was killed in a hunting accident in 987, his successor Hugh Capet ('Capet' because he sported a short cloak called a *cappa*) held just a short strip of territory along the Seine, about 200 kilometres long by 100 wide. Hugh was king but he *ruled* over only a tiny bit of his kingdom. Many of his nobles were richer than he was and a lot more powerful. This was when the holy oil (see page 25) really came in useful. The 'Capetians', as the new dynasty was called, needed all the holy oil they could get.

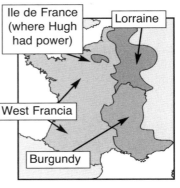

The God of shrieking women

Medieval French people believed in religion in a practical sort of way, like modern people believe in pension funds and taxes: God was real, so were heaven and hell. Hell was obviously something to be avoided and so was purgatory - if possible. Purgatory was an unpleasant holding ground between earth and heaven and all except saints had to spend time there after they died before moving on to heaven or hell. Pilgrimages - visits to holy sites such as the Abbey of St. Denis - bought time off from purgatory so they were a good investment in time and money. Huge numbers went on pilgrimages. Abbot Suger of St. Denis (1081-1151) described the crowds of pilgrims who came to view the saint's relics one particularly busy day in the early twelfth century:

Within the church no one could walk. Women were pressed as in a wine press. They shrieked as though in childbirth ... others to escape death walked on the heads of men as on a continuous floor. The clerics who showed the precious relics were so crushed that they had to escape out of the windows.

Throughout the Middle Ages, religious feeling was extreme. Apart from pilgrimages, the French put vast amounts of time and money into the building of cathedrals and monasteries. During the rebuilding of Chartres Cathedral in the early 1200s after a fire (1194), the faithful unhitched the horses and harnessed themselves to the wagons which carried the stone in order to gain religious merit.

Religious belief was sometimes so intense that believers became confused. They blurred the boundaries between the everyday world and the ideas of their religion. At services of Holy Communion held in the newly-constructed churches, people had visions of the sacred bread actually turning into the body of the Christ-child which the priest then tore apart and offered bleeding to the faithful.

If you're in Chartres

The Cathedral of Notre Dame de Chartres, in Chartres, 88 kilometres southwest of Paris, is one of the greatest of all cathedrals and well worth visiting. Rebuilding after the fire of 1194 took just thirty years, a very short time for such an enormous undertaking given the technology of the period. The wealth of Chartres came from the pilgrims who flocked to see various holy relics, in particular the *Sainte Voile*, the 'Holy Veil', claimed to have been worn by the Virgin Mary while giving birth to Jesus Christ. Miraculously, the Veil,and the income deriving from it, survived the fire.

Chartres Cathedral was rebuilt in the new Gothic style, with pointed arches and large windows to let in the light, a style developed by Abbot Suger of St. Denis when he rebuilt his own abbey 1135-44 after complaining that it wasn't big enough for its crowds of pilgrims. Suger believed that the light in his building reflected the divine light of God.

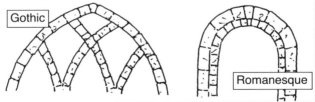

Gothic

Romanesque

Crusades

Pope Urban II (1035-1099) was a spellbinding orator and also, unusually for a Pope, he was French. One summer's

day in 1095 he mounted a wooden platform in a field just outside the city of Clermont in central France. His sermon was to be given in the open air because none of the fifty-four churches of Clermont were big enough for the immense crowd which had gathered to hear him.
He called for a great international campaign by all Christians to liberate Jerusalem and the Holy Land of Palestine from the infidel Muslims who had recently stopped Christian pilgrims from going there. He begged his audience to go to the aid of their Christian brothers and sisters who were suffering under Muslim rule.

'*Deus lo volt!*' roared the crowd: 'God wills it!'

If you're in Clermont Ferrand

The most likely site of the speech of Urban II calling for a crusade is outside the Basilique Notre-Dame-du-Port, northeast of Clermont Cathedral, a beautiful romanesque church which is considerably older than the cathedral.

The crusades were a Europe-wide phenomenon but France was the central player and the Arabs called all western Europeans 'Franks' as a result. Soon after Urban's speech, a motley band of poor, fanatical misfits set out for the east trusting that their faith alone would overcome all obstacles. This 'People's Crusade' was led by two preachers, Peter the Hermit or 'Peterkin', a tiny man on a donkey, and his companion, Walter the Penniless.

The People's Crusade was less an army than a rabble. It was destroyed by the Turks in August 1096, but that same month a well-organised army of 30,000 fighting men, mainly French, set out in four separate detachments, some by land and some by sea. They regrouped at Constantinople (Istanbul), capital of the Eastern Roman Empire, then marched south. The 'First Crusade' was successful. Crusader kingdoms were established in the Holy Land and remained there for over a hundred years.

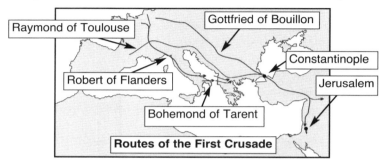

Raymond of Toulouse

Gottfried of Bouillon

Constantinople

Robert of Flanders

Jerusalem

Bohemond of Tarent

Routes of the First Crusade

Feudalism and the 'right of the first night'

France in the Middle Ages was led by its nobility, often of Frankish origin. They were warlike and undisciplined. In the main, only eldest sons inherited land from their fathers which left a large number of younger sons with nothing to do except what nobles were trained to do - fight. A recipe for disorder. The Crusades gave these young men a useful occupation (depending on your point of view) and an opportunity to get rich. When Urban II preached at Clermont, he specifically urged the young warriors in his audience, those who were disturbing the peace (and there were many of them), to vent their fighting spirit usefully by joining his Crusade.

The whole feudal system was geared for war. Knights and lesser nobles swore loyalty to great nobles and undertook to fight for them when required; great nobles swore loyalty to the king and swore to fight and raise troops for him in their turn.

But somebody had to pay for all the armour and the deeds of derring-do. Beneath the knights and nobles were the peasants and serfs who worked the land and owed loyalty and obedience to their lords. It was accepted, by the lords anyway, that the life of serfs was brutish and short. They were tied to the land and were part of its value. In theory they could be divided up. The Lord of Chauvigny, near Nevers on the Loire, owned a serf called Jean Bernard 'whole and undivided' but only a quarter of another serf, Martin Bernard. The other three parts of Martin belonged to the local abbot. Serfs were even obliged to hand over their daughters on their wedding nights so that their lord could have first go, the infamous *jus primae noctis*, or 'right of the first night'.

Knights in armour

Years went by. After a high point early in the twelfth century, the crusader kingdoms lost ground to the native Arabs. The fortress of Acre, last foothold of the crusaders, fell in 1291.

The crusader kingdoms were lost, but the warlike tendencies of the French nobility continued. Unlike their Frankish ancestors of earlier days, French knights fought on horseback on ever more magnificent, specially-bred warhorses or *destriers*. The charge of heavily armoured knights with plumes tossing in the wind and lances lowered was a terrifying experience if you were at the receiving end. They were the tanks of their period and they dominated the battlefields of Europe for several hundred years. By 1340, France, a medieval superpower, could field an army of over 27,000 mounted knights.

And then, at Crécy in northern France on 26 August 1346, the massed nobility of France was slaughtered by a much smaller English army led by the English King, Edward III. What changed things was Edward's troop of longbow men. Longbow arrows could penetrate armour at a range of over 180 metres and trained archers could fire up to twenty arrows per minute. The French knights were slaughtered before they could reach the English lines. Many were too tightly packed together to raise their sword arms when the longbow men moved forward to finish them off. 1,500 French knights died that day.

If you're near Calais

Crécy-en-Ponthieu lies about eighty kilometres due south of Calais. Follow signs marked *Site du Champ du Bataille* to find the battlefield. Edward III directed his forces from a windmill situated at the top of the hill on which he positioned his forces. The site of the windmill, eight hundred metres from the town centre is marked by a wooden *Tour de Guet* (look-out tower).

Hundred Years War

Crécy was the first major land battle of the Hundred Years' War (1337-1453) fought between the kings of England and France. Tension between the two crowns stemmed from the fact that the kings of England were masters in England but subjects in France, because they owed allegiance to the king of France for their lands in his kingdom. This relationship stuck in the throats of the English kings and was displeasing to the French kings also. Matters came to a head in 1328 when Edward III of England laid claim to the French crown for himself.

Edward III claimed the French crown because a new

French king, Philip VI of Valois, had been crowned and Edward didn't think he was entitled. By this time, there was a clear split between the French and the English - most of the French nobles backed Philip's new dynasty, the 'Valois', precisely because the Valois *weren't* English. The French were starting to think of themselves as French - owing loyalty to their country, France, rather than only to their local regions.

Philip VI was a popular choice initially. But before he died in 1350, after defeat at Crécy and after the horrors of the Black Death (1348-9), a plague which wiped out a third of the French population, he wasn't a happy man, to put it mildly, and neither were his subjects. The Valois kings had the misfortune to rule France throughout the entire period of the Hundred Years' War.

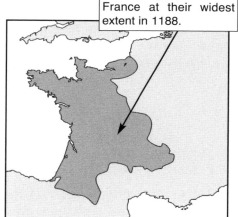

Area of the possessions of the English crown in France at their widest extent in 1188.

If you're in Normandy
Mont St. Michel, near the border with Brittany and just off the Channel coast, was the only strongpoint in western France not to fall to the English during the Hundred Years' War. Topped by its massive Benedictine abbey, it was besieged three times between 1417 and 1433 and withstood each attempt to capture it.

The Maid of Orléans

On a spring day, 6 May 1429, an odd collection of soldiers forced their way out of the beleaguered city of Orléans on the River Loire in central France, under siege by the English for the past six months. Almost unbelievably for the Medieval period, they were led by a girl, a 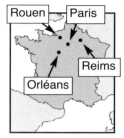 peasant girl dressed in men's clothing. She was armed with a sword. Among her ragbag group of followers were a bastard son of the Duke of Orléans and fighter called Gilles de Rais, also known as 'Bluebeard'. This motley troop led a short, sharp attack on one of the surrounding English forts and took it. Next day they took another. The English soldiers were unused to such determined fighting. By 8 May, the siege was lifted.

Joan of Arc, for it was she, was the seventeen-year-old daughter of a peasant. She was an attractive personality, full of 'courage, tenderness, good sense and earthy humour' as a contemporary described her. By sheer force of personality she had persuaded the future King Charles VII that she was guided by the voices of saints and that they had ordered her to lead French resistance to the English oppressors. They had also ordered her to make sure that Charles was crowned at Reims.

Joan arrived at a bleak moment in French history. By 1429, after nearly a hundred years of the Hundred Years'

War, the English with their Burgundian allies controlled most of northern France including Paris. The English king Henry VI, although only a babe in arms, had been crowned King - of France that is. Joan's victory at Orléans turned the tide and on 17 July that same year, Charles was indeed crowned at Reims, as Joan had promised. The war finally ended in 1453, with a French king, Charles VII, on the French throne and English influence reduced to manageable proportions.

> ### If you're in Reims
> Charles VII was crowned in Reims cathedral on 17 July 1429 with Joan standing nearby and holding her banner, given to her by Charles - a Virgin with a shield and two angels supporting the arms of France on one side and God holding a globe on the other.

Things turned out less happily for Joan. She was captured by the Burgundians in May 1430. They sold her to the English, who tried her as a heretic (peasant girls shouldn't claim to hear saints' voices) at Rouen. There she was condemned to death by burning and the sentence was carried out in May 1430. In 1920, the Pope proclaimed her to be a saint in her own right.

> ### If you're in Rouen
> Joan of Arc was held captive in the *Tour Jeanne d'Arc* during her trial. It's the only survivor of eight towers which once ringed the twelfth-century castle. She was executed in the Rue de Gros Horloge which runs from Rouen Cathedral to the old market. The spot where she was burned is now marked by the *Eglise Jeanne d'Arc*.

ALL CATS LOOK GREY IN THE DARK

CATHOLICS AND PROTESTANTS

<table>
<tr><td colspan="2" align="center">In Brief</td></tr>
<tr><td>1520s</td><td>First French Protestants.</td></tr>
<tr><td>1572</td><td>Saint Bartholomew's Day Massacre.</td></tr>
<tr><td>1589</td><td>End of the Valois, start of the Bourbon Dynasty.</td></tr>
</table>

For whom the bell tolls

In the early hours of 24 August 1572, the bell of Saint Germain de l'Auxerrois in central Paris suddenly split the night air. A signal. Through the dark streets below, Henri the Scarred, Catholic Duke of Guise, led a party of German mercenaries towards the house of Admiral Coligny, senior adviser to King Charles IX. One of the Duke's party forced his way into the Admiral's bedroom. There he stabbed the Admiral to death and threw the bleeding body, still in its night shirt, out of the window and into the courtyard at the Duke's feet.

The Saint Bartholomew's Day massacre had begun.

Admiral Coligny was a Protestant which was why the Duke of Guise hated him. From a Catholic point of view Protestants had become too powerful. The massacre was timed to coincide with the marriage of a Protestant Prince, Henri Bourbon of Navarre, to Margaret, sister of King Charles IX himself - the cream of the French

Protestant nobility were in Paris for the occasion. Guise's plan had been approved by none other than Catherine de Medici (1519-89), queen mother and power behind the throne. Catherine, once charming and rather tolerant, had grown enormously fat and was plagued by indigestion, which may have had something to do with her new-found intolerance.

Protestants were deeply unpopular with the Catholic majority. The bell of Saint Germain let loose hatreds which had been festering for years. Throughout the day, Catholic mobs roamed the streets of Paris, Protestant shops were ransacked and Protestants were hunted down and bludgeoned to death. As many as three thousand were massacred, their bodies tossed into the River Seine. The Pope ordered a special service of thanks to be held in St Peter's, Rome, when he heard the news.

If you're in Blois

The Duke of Guise was murdered in 1588 on the orders of Henri III, successor to Charles IX. Henri had summoned Guise to a royal council meeting in the superb Château of Blois (in the centre of the town). As he entered the council chamber, Guise was told that Henri wanted to see him in Henri's private room or 'closet' before the council meeting. There twenty members of the royal bodyguard lay in wait. Guise was stabbed repeatedly. And once he was well and truly dead, Henri, who'd been hiding behind a tapestry, stepped out to see the body.

In the Palace of the Louvre, young, newly-wed Henri Bourbon and his friend the Prince of Condé were spared the massacre. Charles IX, who'd decided to throw his weight behind the Catholic extremists, ordered the princes brought into his presence and shouted abuse at them but he didn't kill them. They were lucky. Over the coming months more than ten thousand Protestants were murdered in various parts of France.

Hugely unpopular Huguenots
France had escaped the horrors of the Hundred Years' War in the fifteenth century, thanks to the efforts of Joan of Arc, only to be plunged into religious horrors in the sixteenth century.

The international Protestant movement was started by a German monk called Martin Luther in 1517 to 'protest' against abuses by the Catholic Church. It soon spread to France, where Protestants were called Huguenots. The first Huguenot martyr was burned at the stake in Paris in 1523. That was during the reign of Francis I (1515-47) patron of the Italian genius Leonardo da Vinci.

> **If you're in Amboise**
> Francis I spent his childhood at the château of Amboise on the banks of the Loire, as did his sister, Margaret of Navarre, grandmother of Henri Bourbon of Navarre, the future Henri IV. Leonardo da Vinci lived for three years (1516 until his death in 1519) at Le Clos Lucé, a nearby manor house, which has been made into a museum in his honour. It contains models of his inventions.

Persecution did nothing to stop the growth of the Huguenots. They became a powerful minority, attracting members of the nobility as well as merchants and humble tradesmen. And the more they were persecuted, the more fanatical they tended to become. From being *Protestants* some became *Puritans*, seeking to *purify* the Church of anything they didn't agree with. Puritans took to smashing statues and stained-glass windows in churches just as they did in other European countries. In 1562 civil war broke out.

Religious civil war is perhaps the nastiest form of warfare. France suffered from it for many years during the sixteenth century. In 1584, Henri Bourbon of Navarre became heir to the throne and fighting flared up fiercely one last time - because now Catholics faced the dreadful threat of a Protestant king ruling over them. But finally, in 1589, Henri III, the last Valois king of France, was stabbed to death by a fanatical monk, and Henri of Navarre became the rightful king and the first of the Bourbon dynasty.

The Protestants had won.

But had they? The bulk of the population was still Catholic. It took another five years of struggle before Henri could be crowned king of France

- and to do it he had to convert to Catholicism.

All cats look grey in the dark
Henri Bourbon, now Henri IV (ruled 1589-1610), was no religious fanatic whether as a Protestant or a Catholic. Before converting to Catholicism in 1593, legend says that he remarked:

Paris is worth a mass.

He was the best king France ever had. He'd been brought up to live a simple outdoor life, back in Navarre on the Spanish/French border, and he was totally without airs and graces. He wasn't over-clean and he didn't give a fig for smart clothes but he had a terrific sense of humour. Like all Bourbons he was highly sexed. When his mother told him off for his sometimes indiscriminate taste in women, he replied:

Mother, all cats look grey in the dark.

> **If you're in the French Pyrenees**
> Henri IV was born on 13 December 1553 in the Château of Pau, residence of the rulers of Navarre in the 1300s. The Château now houses a museum. Henri's cradle is among the exhibits.

Henri wore his new religion lightly, so lightly that Catholics sometimes wondered whether he'd actually converted to their faith at all. Huguenot leaders were among his top advisers, and in 1598 he authorised the Edict of Nantes which granted all Huguenots religious toleration. Henri set about rebuilding France. He centralised power in his own hands, putting his own chosen men in top positions and keeping the old nobility out. The country knew stability and security for the first time in over sixty years.

It couldn't last. Religious passions were still too inflamed. On the afternoon of 14 May 1610, Henri was travelling in an open coach through the streets of Paris. In the narrow Rue de la Ferronerie his coach was forced to stop by a wine cart and a hay cart which blocked the way. At that moment, a thin, red-headed man leapt onto the coach and stabbed a dagger into Henri's chest, twice. Henri fell back on the cushions. He was dead before they could get him to the Palace of the Louvre.

François Ravaillac, the assassin, was thirty-one years old, half mad and an ardent Catholic. It was getting to be a habit. Henri III and now Henri IV had both been killed by Catholic fanatics. Ravaillac made no attempt to escape. During his execution (he was torn to pieces by horses) he withstood the horrendous pain calmly and without complaint, certain that he'd done the will of God.

WHAT'S THE PLURAL OF LOUIS?

A TOUCH OF CLASS

The four Louissss ...

For most of the seventeenth and eighteenth centuries, France was ruled by four kings called Louis. Three of them were feeble and one of them was strong.

Louis XIII	(reigned 1610-43) - feeble.
Louis XIV	(reigned 1643-1715) - strong.
Louis XV	(reigned 1715-1774) - feeble.
Louis XVI	(reigned 1774-1793) - feeble.

The Red Eminence

Cardinal Richelieu, *de facto* ruler of France 1624-42 while Louis XIII was king, had fourteen cats. They had a special room next to his bedroom and two attendants and they were fed on chicken paté twice a day. Among them were Ludoviska (a Polish cat), Ludovic le Cruel and Soumise (his favourite).

Ludoviska, Ludovic, Soumise and the others were about the only creatures who weren't frightened of Cardinal Richelieu. Colleagues feared him almost as much as did his enemies. He kept spies in most of the fashionable drawing rooms of Paris and he knew exactly what everyone was saying about him. Even King Louis XIII quailed in his presence. Known as the 'Red Eminence' because of his red cardinal's robes, Richelieu was sternness personified. Even princes of the royal blood gave way to him.

Richelieu was powerful because his king, Louis XIII, was weak. Louis, son of Henri IV, had been crowned in 1610 when he was only eight and for a while his mother, Marie de Medici, ran the country - before Richelieu took over. Richelieu, from a poor but noble family, was chaplain to young Louis's bride-to-be, Anne of Austria. As such he was part of the royal household. Ambitious and very clever, by 1622 the 'Red Eminence' was a cardinal, the highest rank in the Catholic Church below the Pope. Marie was sidelined, much to her annoyance. In 1624, Richelieu became Louis's Chief Minister.

Louis disliked Richelieu but he needed him because Richelieu was so incredibly smart - and incredibly ruthless. Richelieu always put France first, even ahead of his religion. In 1635 he took France into the horrendously destructive Thirty Years' War (1618-1648) on the side of Protestant England, Holland and Sweden and against the Catholic Spanish Empire, because he thought this was in French interests, Spain then being the world superpower.

The Sun King
Richelieu died in 1642 at the age of fifty-seven. Louis XIII died a year later. The new king, Louis XIV, was only five but he was a very different person to his feeble father. He reigned for seventy-two years.

During Louis XIV's childhood, France was nearly torn apart by a series of bloody uprisings of the nobility, uprisings known collectively as the 'Fronde'. At the age of ten, he had to leave Paris for his own safety. His Chief Minister, an Italian Cardinal called Mazarin, also Louis's mother's lover, eventually crushed the rebellion. But that taste of danger stayed with Louis for the rest of his life.

When Mazarin died in 1661, Louis immediately took up the reins of power. This was a shock to everybody because he was so very different to his father. He immediately set out to weaken the nobility who'd caused him so much trouble during the *Fronde*. His plan was to keep them away from their estates and somewhere where he could keep an eye on them.

At the Palace of Versailles.
The day of a court lady at the Palace of Versailles in 1670:

Early morning: off hunting, then back to the Palace and change into court dress.
Late morning: possibly attend the Queen's toilet (hair, make-up, getting dressed etc.), Mass then dinner.
3.00-7.00pm: to the grand reception rooms with all the royal family, the royal mistresses and most of the court, everyone wandering from room to room or gambling at the gaming tables, a band plays all the time.
7.00-10.00pm: into coaches then onto gondolas on the canal, 1.6 kilometres long in the Palace gardens, more music.
10.00pm: back to the Palace to watch a comedy by Molière or a tragedy by Racine.
12.00pm: supper.
12.00pm-3.00am: a ball.

Life at the Palace of Versailles was *exhausting*. It was meant to be. Starting in 1661, the Palace was built by Louis XIV for the grandeur of his crown and also to house the noblility and to keep them occupied. Trapped in

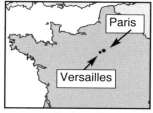

an endless whirl of entertainment and deadly court etiquette, the poor things had no time to cause trouble and no time to go back to their estates to cause it, except possibly once a year out of season. The exotic, almost-sad quality of aristocratic life in this period is perfectly captured by the artist Antoine Watteau in his exquisite paintings of *Fêtes galantes*, picnic parties of noble ladies and gentlemen in vaguely rural dress which became very popular towards the end of the century. Watteau's *Fêtes galantes* paintings aren't actually of Versailles but they perfectly catch its atmosphere.

Versailles

From the start, Versailles was designed to be the grandest palace in Europe and the focal point of all France. One of its chief architects was Jules Hardouin-Mansart, great nephew of François Mansart (1598-1666) who invented the double pitched 'Mansard' roof so typical of French *châteaux* (castles).

Mansart wasn't cheap. He was quite capable of tearing one of his buildings down and starting again if he didn't like it, and billing his customer for both of them. But even without him Versailles would have cost a fortune. When completed it had (approximately) 10,000 rooms, many of them enormous. The famous Hall of Mirrors is over eighty metres long. Outside there were fabulous gardens. The extravagance was incredible. Around the Trianon, a private residence of the royal family but part of the complex, the summer bedding plants were changed every day. In season, the scent of the tuber roses was so strong that people had to retreat indoors.

Versailles was never a family home, not with 10,000 rooms, hence the Trianon for a bit of privacy. It was more of a town, a sprawling, crowded sort of place open to the public who were allowed in to watch the king eat. By 1684, seven thousand members of the nobility were living there on and off together with their attendants and hangers on, often in very uncomfortable quarters. It got so crowded that, in 1700, the Swiss Guard was ordered to clear beggars from the passages.

If you're in Paris
The small town of Versailles and its palace are within easy reach of central Paris by train or metro. The whole complex including the gardens and the Trianon is vast.

The Sun King and the Sun King's women

Louis was given the nickname 'Sun King' because when he was young he once dressed up as the Sun for a ballet. He later chose the Sun as his personal emblem. Like his grandfather Henri IV, he had a good sense of humour and beautiful manners. He would even take his hat off to chambermaids.

Speaking of chambermaids, like all Bourbons, Louis was highly sexed. In 1658, he married Marie Thérèse, a Spanish princess who adored him, but he had many lovers on the side as well, including the infamous Madame de Montespan. Montespan bore him six children and their affair went on for years, growing more tempestuous with each year. The final falling out came in 1679 when she was found to be closely involved with a witch. Her parting shot:

I may have many faults in my person, but at any rate I do not smell as nasty as you do.

If you're near Biarritz

Louis XIV and his bride Marie Thérèse were married in 1660 in the splendid Eglise St. Jean Baptiste in the small resort of St. Jean de Luz in the Basque country. The ceremony completed, the couple left via the south door which has been sealed ever since, symbolising friendship between France and Spain. The house in town, 'Maison Louis XIV', where Louis lived in the weeks before his marriage, is also worth visiting and is open to the public.

By that time, Louis was interested in his children's governess, Madame Scarron, a friend of Montespan and a rather pious widow but extremely beautiful. She was made the Marquise de Maintenon in 1679 as a sign of his affection and, sometime after the death of poor Marie Thérèse (1683), Maintenon and Louis were secretly married. It was a happy match although Louis was demanding. When both were in their seventies, she complained that he still wanted his conjugal rights up to three times a day.

Despite his love of dancing and his numerous affairs, Louis XIV was far from frivolous. He worked an average eight-hour day, delving into all kinds of details, and he alone made decisions on all important matters. Every week, a detailed balance sheet showing the national finances was presented to him. Like his grandfather, he preferred to surround himself with talented men from less than noble backgrounds, men such as Jean Colbert, a draper's son, previously Mazarin's secretary, who became his finance minister and general right-hand man.

Because of Louis XIV, France became the most powerful country in Europe once more. It already had the largest population. Taxes were reformed, industries were encouraged. There were drawbacks however. Louis was a staunch Catholic. In 1685 he revoked the Edict of Nantes and launched a life-long persecution of the Huguenots. Since Huguenots were among the most hard-working people in France, this boded ill for the future.

If you're in Languedoc

After the revocation of the Edict of Nantes in 1685, many Huguenots emigrated to Protestant countries but some hid out in the wilderness of the Cévennes. From there they conducted a guerrila war of resistance against the French army. They're known to history as the 'Camisards', because they fought in their shirts (*camis*) being without proper resources. The leader of the resistance was a young man called Roland who was born at Le Mas Soubeyran near the village of Mialet, northwest of Nîmes. It's now the Musée du Desert, open from March through to November. It focuses on the Revolt of the Camisards and other aspects of French Protestantism.

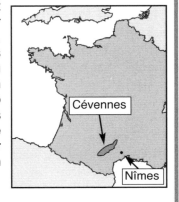

Attention please!

Apart from religion, Louis's other weak point was war. He built up a magnificent army, helped by men such as Colonel Martinet, who improved discipline and, perhaps unfairly, became a byword for petty strictness. Louis's first target was Holland, which he loathed because it was Protestant and because it was a republic. He invaded it in 1667, and again in 1672. Then in 1689 he went to war against the German Emperor Leopold I. In each case, the gains he made for France weren't worth the cost. War was ruinously expensive.

Finally, in 1701, came the War of the Spanish Succession, fought over who should be the next king of Spain. England and most of Europe were on one side, France was on the other. France suffered a string of humiliating defeats. In the Treaties of Utrecht (1713-14) which ended the war, it was agreed that Louis's grandson should be the next king of Spain, but in most other respects France was the loser.

By then, Louis XIV was an old man and bald as a coot, although he didn't show it. Back in 1683, when he'd discovered that he was going bald, he'd had his head shaved and taken to wearing a wig - thus starting a fashion all over Europe which lasted for the next hundred years.

I'm pining for 'yew'

Thirty years after Louis XIV died (1715), in February 1745, there was a masked ball at the Palace of Versailles. The most beautiful woman in a sea of beautiful women was gorgeous Jeanne-Antoinette d'Etoiles, dressed as Diana the Huntress. She was absolutely stunning. The previous evening, at yet another ball, she'd danced for the first time with Louis XV, successor to Louis XIV, and he'd been bowled over by her beauty. Unfortunately, tonight Louis didn't show up until two in the morning and when he did, he was dressed as a yew tree from the park of Versailles, of all things - along with seven other yew trees.

The only way she could tell which one was him was by how often his particular tree kept looking in her direction. From this unlikely beginning began one of the best known royal affairs in history. Jeanne-Antoinette was made the Marquise de Pompadour, the name by which she's best known. By September she was the king's official mistress, which she remained until her death.

Louis XV got the nickname *Bien-aimé*, or 'Well-Beloved' when he was a child. Like Louis XIV, who was his great-grandfather, he came to the throne when he was only five; unlike Louis XIV he was lazy and easily influenced and he certainly didn't live up to his nickname. For many years, Madame Pompadour was the power behind the throne. She put her favourites in important positions, and in 1756 persuaded Louis to take France into the Seven Years' War (1756-63). As a result of this adventure, France lost most of her colonies and outposts in India and North America to the growing British Empire.

Seven Years' War

The Seven Years' War (1756-63) was fought between Britain, Prussia and Hanover on one side and France, Russia, Austria and Spain on the other. It was about who should dominate Germany - and who should dominate the world beyond Europe.

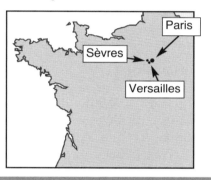
Louis XV retreated from government. Pompadour wasn't the first of his mistresses and she wasn't the last. He spent more and more time with them. The last was the Comtesse du Barri, previously a shop assistant named Marie Bécu, who caught his eye in 1768. Marie had worked as a high-class call girl and her mentor, Jean du Barri, known as 'Mahomet' because he kept so many girls, became her brother-in-law. She married his brother, the Comte du Barri, at the king's request, thus gaining her title. In those days, the king's official mistress had to be married - married women were permitted more freedom than unmarried women.

Du Barri spent money like water, this at a time when the poor were desperately poor. Among other extravagancies, she commissioned incredibly expensive dinner services from Pompadour's factory at Sèvres and employed the artist Jean-Honoré Fragonard to decorate her Pavilion at Louveciennes.

If you're in Paris

Louis XV gave the small Château de Louveciennes, to the west of Versailles, to Madame de Barri. She built the Pavilion nearby to provide larger reception rooms. It's a beautiful neoclassical building, The Fragonard paintings are now in the Frick museum in New York and the Pavilion has had to make do with copies - but it's still beautiful.

Philosophically speaking ...

The Eighteenth Century was a gilded age, but the gilt wore increasingly thin. While kings and aristocrats danced at Versailles and the poor got poorer, a group of thinking men set out to show how things could be done differently. They were known as the *'Philosophes'*, a varied bunch of scientists, writers and other thinkers, who believed that human reason leads to progress and that superstition and tradition lead to decay.

Most famous of the *Philosophes* was Voltaire (1694-1778). Voltaire was born during the reign of Louis XIV and grew up during the horrific persecution of the Huguenots brought on by Louis's revocation of the Edict of Nantes in 1685. Intolerance revolted him. In later life he habitually referred to the Catholic Church as *l'Infame* (the Vile). He himself was a deist believing in a God of 'Reason'.

At the age of thirty-two, Voltaire was whisked away to

England following a quarrel with a powerful nobleman. There he discovered the English language, Shakespeare, parliamentary government, freedom of the press, and the science of Isaac Newton. On his return in 1728, he began to preach these virtues. He was a brilliant writer. Even kings took notice of what he had to say - although not Louis XV.

The ideas of the *Philosophes* were put together in a massive work of scholarship called the *Encyclopedie*, published in Paris in thirty-five volumes starting in 1751. It was both an encyclopaedia and a call for major political reform. As a result, its editor Denis Diderot lived in almost constant danger of imprisonment by the authorities. On one occasion he was even protected by Pompadour - royal mistresses weren't *all* bad.

Almost the last Louis

Louis XV died in 1774 and his son Louis XVI (ruled 1774-1793, the last bit in prison) inherited a shaky throne. Louis XVI was well-meaning but limited in his outlook. His hobby was making clocks. During his disastrous reign, backward-looking aristocrats blocked all reform. Food riots and other disorders flared up again and again.

Louis XVI's government was constantly in need of money but when his finance minister Anne Turgot (a man, despite his name) suggested a tax on large estates, the aristocrats dug their heels in and Louis was too weak and undecided to stand up to them. Turgot was sacked. Meanwhile Louis's wife, the Austrian princess Marie-Antoinette, dressed up as a milkmaid and threw extravagant 'rustic' parties in the gardens of Versailles -

an inspired way to make herself popular when real milkmaids were living in abject poverty.

Times were about to change. The milkmaids were about to get their own back.

If you're in Paris, near Chantilly

It wasn't only Marie-Antoinette who played at being a milkmaid. It was a fashionable thing to do among aristocratic ladies of the period. The *Hameau* of the Château of Chantilly, near the town of that name about 45 kilometres north of Paris, is a mock eighteenth-century rustic village. It was the model for Marie-Antoinette's *Hameau* in the gardens of the Palace of Versailles. Sweetened, whipped cream from the Chantilly cows became a well-known delicacy - *crème chantilly*.

MADAME GUILLOTINE
THE FRENCH REVOLUTION

In Brief - the Revolution	
May 1789	Estates General meets.
June 1789	Oath of the Tennis Court.
July 1789	Fall of the Bastille.
June 1791	Louis XVI flees Paris.
September 1792	Battle of Valmy.
January 1793	Execution of Louis XVI.
April 1793 -	
July 1794	The Terror.
July 1794	Fall of Robespierre.

Estates General

In 1788, stormy financial waters were threatening to drown the government of Louis XVI. Backward-looking aristocrats and others blocked all attempts at financial reform. These powerful men forced Louis to call an assembly of the 'Estates General', a traditional gathering of representatives from the three 'estates' of society: nobles, clergy and commons. The last such assembly had been called in 1614 by Marie de Medici, so this was a major event.

Representatives of the Three Estates poured into Versailles from all over France. Among them was Maximilien Robespierre, a slight, dapper young lawyer who had been elected as deputy for the commons of Arras in northern France. Arriving at Versailles in May 1789 along with other deputies to the Estates General, Robespierre found cheap accommodation at an inn in the town and immediately plunged into frenzied political activity, speaking in public whenever he got the opportunity. He was a follower of the ideas of the *philosophe* Jean Jacques Rousseau. Rousseau had argued that it was 'society' which made people corrupt and not the other way around. Therefore, according to Rousseau and his followers, what was needed was a perfect society and then all would be well. Which seemed harmless enough - until Robespierre tried to put theory into practice. Robespierre's later, well-earned reputation for bloodthirsty ruthlessness sprang from good intentions.

If you're in Arras
9 rue Maximilien Robespierre in the town of Arras in northern France is where Robespierre lived before moving to Versailles in 1789. Admission is free and there's an exhibition of traditional building skills.

Time for tennis
The wealthy nobles and other citizens who had demanded an Assembly in order to protect their own privileges had no idea what they were letting themselves in for. They were turkeys who'd just voted for Christmas.

Once the representatives of the three estates were gathered at Versailles, an argument broke out over whether votes should be equal between them, in which case the nobles and clergy would have a built-in majority, or on the basis of one vote per deputy in which case the commons would dominate. (There were six hundred deputies representing the commons to three hundred each for the nobles and clergy.) With support from parish priests and a few forward-thinking noblemen, the latter voting method favoured the commons. Nobles and clergy dug their heels in.

Fired up by the progressive ideas of the *philosophes*, and

since they already represented 98% of the French people, the commons declared themselves to be a 'National Assembly' which the other two estates were welcome to join if they wanted to - or not if they didn't. On 20 June 1789, finding themselves locked out of their meeting hall and believing that the king was about to order them to go home, the commons adjourned to an indoor tennis court at the suggestion of one of their members, Dr. Joseph Guillotin*. There they swore the famous 'tennis-court oath' never to disband until France had a proper, written constitution. A week later, Louis caved in. A 'National Constituent Assembly' was born.

Revolution!

That summer, hopes and fears ran incredibly high. In Paris the poor working class, contemptuously referred to as *sans-culottes* ('no knee-breeches') by the wealthy, expected wonders from the new Assembly. But then a 'Great Fear' spread among them that the king was gathering troops to suppress the Assembly. On 14 July 1789 on a warm, cloudy afternoon, a mob stormed the ancient prison/fortress of the Bastille in central Paris believing it to contain political prisoners. Once they'd broken in, they found that it contained only four prisoners, none of them political, but the damage was

*On 1 December 1789, Dr Guillotin proposed that all executions should be 'by means of a machine'. This was so as to make executions less painful for the victims and so that decapitation would no longer be a privilege reserved for the nobility. The 'guillotine' was actually designed by a surgeon called Antoine Louis. After experiments on dead bodies, it was first used in earnest in 1792.

done. The commander and some of his men were killed and the Bastille was burned to the ground.

The Revolution proper, the bloody bit, had started.

> **If you're in Paris**
> There's nothing left of the Fortress of Bastille. Bastille today is a roundabout and a Metro station. However, before attacking the Bastille, the revolutionary mob broke into the Hôtel des Invalides (metro La Tour Maubourg or Varenne and open to the public), built by Louis XIV in the 1670s to house disabled soldiers. After bitter fighting, the revolutionaries seized 28,000 rifles from an underground storehouse and then headed for the Bastille.

Sparked by the fall of the Bastille, poor peasants in the countryside rose up in revolt. Châteaux were ransacked, landlords and priests were murdered, crops were pillaged. Back at the Assembly, the rich and powerful panicked. On 4 August, they abolished serfdom and all feudal dues left over from the Middle Ages. On 26 August a 'Declaration of the Rights of Man and of the Citizen' proclaimed liberty and equality for all citizens. Louis, hopeless as ever, refused to agree to it.

Meanwhile the ecomic situation grew worse. In Paris the extreme poor were near starvation. On 5 October, a mob of around six thousand lower class women, including prostitutes and other unfortunates, marched the nineteen kilometres from Paris to Versailles in driving rain shouting 'Bread! Bread!' and *'Vive la nation!'* Once at Versailles they camped out in the courtyards and refused to leave without the royal family. They believed that the King was basically well meaning but that at Versailles he was surrounded by bad advisers. Louis agreed to sign the

Declaration of the Rights of Man but it was too late. Next day, Louis, Marie-Antoinette and their children were taken back to Paris by the women, some of them riding triumphantly on the barrels of captured cannon and others screaming abuse at the unpopular Queen. The royal family were housed in the Palace of the Tuileries, effectively captives.

The Assembly followed the King to Paris, there being no point in staying at Versailles without him. It held its meetings in the Riding School at the Tuileries. Robespierre found shared lodgings nearby.

Jacobins

Over the next two years, the face of France was utterly changed. Feudal dues had already gone. Now the old geographical regions were abolished and the country was organised into its present modern departments, cantons and communes with elected local governments. Church property was nationalised and much of it was redistributed to the peasants.

Meanwhile, political parties were formed, some arguing for greater reform, some for less. Our political terms 'left' and 'right' come from that time. To start with, the moderates, called the Girondins, were in power. They sat towards the middle of the semi-circular Assembly. Ranged against them were the old guard on the right and the radicals on the left. The biggest radical party was the party of the Jacobins, called after a former convent where they held their private debates. Robespierre, by now a well-known figure, soon dominated the Jacobins, arguing in favour of further reforms for the underprivileged.

It was all too much for Louis, a virtual prisoner in the Tuileries Palace, next door to the Louvre. On June 1791, he and his family fled Paris at night, their coach rattling over the moonlit cobblestones. They headed for the coast, but were caught at Varennes and forced to return. Now they really were prisoners and a new, more angry wind began to blow. That September the Constituent Assembly was dissolved and a new 'Legislative Assembly' took its place. A crowd watched in silence as the deputies left. Only when Robespierre appeared did they burst into applause. There was no doubt who was the hero of the hour. Some onlookers undid his horses and harnessed themselves to his coach to honour him.

War!

France had become a danger to other European governments which were still monarchies. Their rulers began to make very threatening noises. To head off the threat, on 20 April 1792, France declared war on Austria and Prussia which were the most menacing. This was a hasty decision and very dangerous. A month or two later, professional Austrian and Prussian troops crossed the French border, sweeping the French army to one side. They marched towards Paris.

On the streets of Paris, excitement and fear were intense. Anyone suspected of sympathising with the enemies of the Revolution, meaning pretty well anyone with noble blood, was liable to be arrested and put in prison. That August, volunteers joined the army in droves. Suspecting that Louis was on the side of the enemy, a panic-stricken mob stormed the Tuileries, captured the royal family and locked them in the medieval Temple Prison in far worse conditions than before and where there was no chance of escape. Shortly after, there was an appalling general massacre in the prisons. Fanatical *sans-culottes* butchered 1,200 royalist prisoners (although not the King and his family). The killings went on for four days. There were reports of cannibalism and rape and the authorities were powerless to stop it. Finally, having secured their backs and to everyone's great relief, the bloody mob marched off to join their comrades in the army. Their fanatical determination was decisive. At the Battle of Valmy on 20 September, France won a great victory against the armies of Prussia and Austria and the Revolution was safe - for the time being.

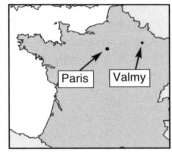

Men of the Mountain

The Battle of Valmy was a turning point. Revolutionary frenzy reached a peak. The new governing body was to be a 'National Convention'. It was dominated by the *Montaignards*, 'Men of the Mountain', so called because they sat on the highest benches. These were the most radical revolutionaries, mainly Jacobins, Robespierre among them. The National Convention immediately proclaimed that France was now a Republic - leaving open for the time being the question of what to do with prisoner 'Louis Capet*' previously known as Louis XVI.

There followed some of the most extraordinary months in human history. The revolutionaries set out to wipe the slate clean:

*The Bourbon dynasty were descended from the the Capetian dynasty via the Valois.

In October 1793 a new revolutionary calendar was declared. There would be twelve months, each of three ten-day weeks, making 360 days in all. Every tenth day would be a day of rest to replace Sunday. The remaining five or six days of the year were to be *jours complementaires* (free days) and were to be feast days. The first day of Year One of the new calendar, 1 Vendémiaire, was set retrospectively at 22 September 1792, the start of the Republic. The calendar remained in force until 1 January 1806 when the traditional calendar was reinstated by Napoleon.

The Republican Calendar

The names of the months of the Republican Calendar were largely the work of the poet and playwright Philip-François d'Eglantine who sat in the National Convention and was on the Calendar Committee. On 12 January 1794, he was arrested on false charges of forgery and was guillotined that April. On his way to the scaffold he was very calm and gave out copies of his poems to the crowd.

January	Pluviôse (month of rain)
February	Ventôse (month of winds)
March	Germinal (month of seeds)
April	Floréal (month of blossom)
May	Prairial (month of pasture)
June	Messidor (month of harvest)
July	Thermidor (month of heat)
August	Fructidor (month of fruits)
September	Vendémiaire (month of vintage)
October	Brumaire (month of fog)
November	Frimaire (month of hoar frost)
December	Nivôse (month of snow)

✓ There was also to be a ten-hour clock - a hundred minutes to the hour and a hundred seconds to the minute - 100,000 seconds per day. This idea never really took off.

✓ The Church was to be abolished. On 7 November, a Feast of the God of Reason was celebrated in the Cathedral of Notre Dame with all due pomp and ceremony.

✓ Pensions were introduced for poor families.

✓ Free primary education was organised.

✓ Meanwhile, the Academy of Science was looking into a metric system for measures. On the committee was the brilliant scientist Antoine Lavoisier, founder of modern chemistry. The metric system, finally adopted in 1794, has proved to be the most far-reaching of all the revolutionary reforms.

If you're in Paris

The Musée du Louvre by the north bank of the River Seine was originally a royal palace and fortress, begun in the thirteenth century and rebuilt in the sixteenth century. It was opened as a public museum, the *Musée de la Revolution* by order of the National Convention on 10 August 1793. (The idea for a museum had first been proposed by Louis XVI.) At that time it contained the Royal collection of around 2,500 paintings but it's since grown to over 30,000 paintings and other exhibits. Admission is free on the first Sunday of every month.

The Terror

While these extraordinary and optimistic reforms were being put in place, the revolution continued to show its darker side.

On the morning of 21 January 1793 a closely guarded carriage entered the Place Louis XV, soon to be called the Place de la Concorde. A huge crowd had gathered. The people watched in total silence as Louis XVI was taken from the carriage and his hands were tied together by the executioners. Then, still in silence, he was led up the steps to the guillotine. A roll of drums started up. It drowned any chance he might have had of making a speech. At 10.15 *am* the blade fell. One of the executioners seized the head by the hair and held it up for all to see.

'Long live the Republic!' shouted the crowd.

If you're in Paris

The guillotine used for the execution of Louis XVI was set up in the northwest corner of what is now the Place de la Concorde, close to where the statue of Brest now stands. Further executions, including the execution of Queen Marie-Antoinette, were carried out on the other side of the Place, on a guillotine set up close to the entrance to the Jardin des Tuileries.

In an atmosphere of wartime paranoia, on 6 April 1793 a 'Committee of Public Safety' was formed. This sinister body formed a sort of government behind the government. It had nine members including Robespierre and a Jacobin leader called Georges Danton, an ex-lawyer with a booming voice and big, black eyebrows. Under Danton's influence the Committee was relatively restrained but then Robespierre took over. Robespierre did not invent the Great Terror which followed but he was a leading figure. Louis XVI was one among a great many who died. By the summer of 1794, 300,000 people had been arrested, and up to 20,000 in Paris and 40,000 elsewhere in France had gone to the guillotine. Among them were Danton himself, executed on 30 March, and Antoine Lavoisier, executed on 8 May 1794. As the arresting officer put it:

The Revolution has no need of scientists.

At the rate of thirty a day on average in Paris, the executions were exceptional popular entertainment. Some old women used to claim their places early. They were known as *les Tricoteuses* (the knitters) because they took their knitting.

If you're in Paris

The main prison during the Reign of Terror was the Conciergerie (metro Cité), a fourteenth-century palace. It was conveniently close to the Palais de la Justice next door, where the Revolutionary Tribunal sat in judgement. Between January 1793 and July 1794, over 2,500 prisoners were kept in its dungeons before being sent to their deaths, including Queen Marie-Antoinette who was kept there in a room by herself in August 1793. Her room is now a chapel but can be visited.

Rob gets the chop

Eventually even Robespierre grew tired of the carnage and concluded that there was no point to it any longer. He was especially critical of the travelling tribunals sent out to suppress dissent in the regions. These tribunals took mobile guillotines with them on carts. Some were little better than travelling abbatoirs. On 26 July 1794, he spoke out against going on with the Terror and threatened punishment for those who had gone too far.

Seeing that the great man appeared to have had a change of heart, Robespierre's fellow members on the Committee realised that they would have to act swiftly or they themselves would be next for the chop. The following day, supporters of Robespierre were shouted down in the Convention and, in the afternoon, Robespierre, his brother Augustin and three others were arrested. Robespierre was taken to prison but then freed by his supporters and taken to the *Hotel de Ville*, the Paris town hall. He was shot in the jaw when troops later effected his recapture. He spent the night in great pain.

Next day, 28 July 1794, Robespierre was executed in the Place de la Révolution (modern Place de la Concorde) before a large, jeering crowd. The 'Incorruptible', as he had been known, was in agony when he stepped up to the guillotine. In the words of a fellow revolutionary, Pierre Vergniaud, executed the previous year:

> *The Revolution is like Saturn*. She devours her own children.*

After Robespierre's execution, the Revolution began to burn itself out. People had had enough excitement. In October 1795, the Convention abolished itself. A new

---

*Saturn was a Roman god linked to the earlier Greek god Cronus, god of agriculture among other things. Cronus castrated his father, married his own sister and then ate their children. He'd been warned that he would be overthrown by one of his offspring - as he was, by Zeus who was born later.

'Directory' of five members was appointed to run the country with separate law-making chambers: the 'Council of the Ancients' and the 'Council of Five Hundred'. The new members of the Directory weren't very revolutionary but they weren't royalist either. They tended to be just plain greedy. It was fashionable to be rich again.

a rich person

THE LITTLE CORPORAL
NAPOLEON BONAPARTE

In brief: Napoleon takes over, 1795-1799

1795	Directory established.
1796	Napoleon given command of French army in Italy.
1798	Napoleon asked to prepare for an invasion of Britain. Says it can't be done while Britain commands the sea. Prepares for invasion of Egypt instead.
1798	Napoleon conquers Egypt in order to weaken Britain by putting pressure on British colonies further east.
1798	French fleet destroyed by Admiral Nelson at the Battle of the Nile.
1799	Napoleon returns to France and seizes power.

A journey by moonlight

Robespierre had gone and the Directory had come, but the war with Britain and other countries opposed to the Revolution still dragged on.

On 23 August 1799, in the relative cool of the early hours of the morning, if you'd been standing on the quayside of the Egyptian port of Alexandria, you'd have seen two fast frigates slip silently out of the harbour into the warm, moonlit waters of the Mediterranean. On board the lead ship was Napoleon Bonaparte, commander of the French forces in Egypt, heading back to France. His journey was a gamble. The previous summer, the French fleet had been destroyed by the British under Admiral Nelson at the Battle of the Nile. The French army in Egypt was stranded. British naval patrols were everywhere.

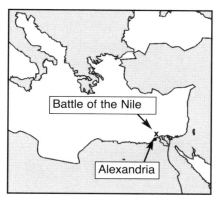

Somehow, by some miracle, Napoleon's tiny flotilla avoided contact with British ships as it made its way across the Mediterranean. He landed safely at Fréjus on the south coast of France six weeks later. By 16 October he was in Paris where he found the Directory lurching towards yet another crisis. On 9 November 1799, he seized power.

> **If you're in Provence**
> Fréjus is a charming small town on the coast between Nice and Toulon, first settled by Greeks from Marseille and then a Roman town, *Forum Julii*. Fréjus was also a landing point for Allied troops in August 1944.

First Consul

Having dumped the Directory, Napoleon became 'First Consul' of the Republic. There were two other consuls under the new arrangement but he was the only one that mattered.

Napoleon Bonaparte (1769-1821) was a truly extraordinary man. From fairly modest origins in Corsica he had risen to become absolute ruler of France and he was still only thirty. Even when on campaign he never stopped working. He slept in his blue and white campaign tent which had two 'rooms': a 'bedroom' and an 'office'. If there was a lot of work to get through, he might start as early as two in the morning. Secretaries wilted at the pace.

During fifteen years in power, a ceaseless flow of orders and letters flowed from Napoleon's desk. He's reckoned to have dictated as many as 80,000 documents, an average of nearly fifteen orders or letters per day, many of them very important. On top of that, there were endless meetings, receptions, ceremonial occasions - and, of course, battles.

Napoleon put his stamp on France, and indeed on Europe, like no other individual before or after. Basically, he took the reforms of the Revolution (except the democratic ones) and made them work. From education to local government to the law (the 'Code Napoleon', the basic codification of French law, is named in his honour), all facets of French life bear the mark of his attention. For instance, the modern system of *lycées* and *écoles secondaires* in secondary education was begun by him.

Given his work load it's remarkable that Napoleon found time for the pleasures of life, but he did. He married Josephine Beauharnais, a widow and the daughter of a West Indian landowner, on 9 March 1796 when he was twenty-six and she was thirty-one. She took fours years off her age on the marriage certificate and he added eighteen months to his. She was lovely and lively, if not very faithful, but then, neither was he. They stayed fond of each even after he divorced her in 1810.

Peace at last

On 18 April 1802, an Easter Sunday, a long and rather tattered procession of hired cabs and worn-out state coaches made its way through the streets of Paris towards Notre Dame for a service of thanksgiving for peace with Britain. The long war to protect the gains of the Revolution was finally over - the Treaty of Amiens had been ratified the day before. This procession was nothing like the glittering state processions of former days and the men in the coaches were nothing like the bejewelled courtiers of old. They were Napoleon's men, battle-hardened generals and hard-working officials

every one of them. Many had no time for ceremony nor for religion. They were just going through the motions because Napoleon, who headed the procession, insisted. But then, he had little time for religion either, except in so far as it was useful.

The French had reason to be grateful for the Treaty of Amiens. Western Europe was at last at peace, and France was the master of Europe. That August, after a referendum of three million votes, Napoleon was made 'Consul for Life'. Now no-one could shift him.

If you're in Corsica

Maison Bonaparte, where Napoleon was born, is in rue St-Charles, in the old Genoese part of the city of Ajaccio. It's now a museum dedicated to the Bonaparte family and houses a collection of Bonaparte memorabilia. Napoleon stayed there for five days on his return from Egypt in 1799, the last time he was on Corsican soil. The house was badly damaged by Corsican nationalists in 1793, but rebuilt on Napoleon's orders shortly after.

Emperor of war balloons

After the Treaty of Amiens, France was certainly the master of Europe, but other Europeans weren't happy about it. Both sides began to break the provisions of the Treaty. War between France and Britain broke out again in 1803 and Napoleon assembled a massive invasion force on the Channel coast intending to crush his meddlesome neighbour once and for all. Some of the suggestions for getting this force across the Channel sound like pure science fiction.  Two Frenchmen, the Montgolfier brothers, had invented the hot-air balloon back in 1783. Now plans were considered for vast balloons with platforms large enough to carry up to 3,000 soldiers at a time. Other suggestions included a raft over 800 metres long, propelled by windmills and horse-mills and capable of carrying up to 50,000 men.

Napoleon had become a slave to his own ambition. As if plans for giant balloons were not enough, in 1804 he was crowned 'Emperor' in Notre Dame, placing the crown on his own head to show that he owed it to no one. European reformers were horrified. Was it for this that so many had died during the Revolution? The Austrian composer Beethoven scratched Napoleon's name from the dedication of his *Eroica* symphony on hearing the news. And pride was followed by a fall - next year, on 2 August 1805, the combined French and Spanish fleets (at that time fighting as allies) were shattered by the British at Trafalgar off the Spanish coast.

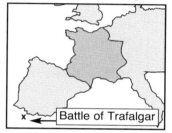

Battle of Trafalgar

Invasion of Britain became impossible after Trafalgar. To make matters worse, Russia, Sweden and Austria joined the war against France again. Bowing his head to the obvious, Napoleon turned his back on the sea and headed east, leaving only a skeleton invasion force behind him. Now he showed his extraordinary military genius. First, he defeated the combined might of the Russians and Austrians at the Battle of Austerlitz (2 December 1805), in what is now the Czech Republic. Next, he defeated Prussia at the Battles of Jena and Auerstadt (both on 14 October 1806). Finally, on a tented raft moored in the middle of the River Niemen on the border between Russia and Poland, he signed the Treaty of Tilsit with the Russian Tsar Alexander I, agreeing on how they would carve up Europe between them (25 June 1807).

He'd done it again. Once again, of the major powers, only Britain was still fighting.

In brief: Napoleon's glory days 1800-1807

1800   Napoleon defeats Austrians at the Battle of Marengo.
1801   Austrians sign another peace treaty.
1802   Treaty of Amiens signed between Britain and France.
1802   Napoleon made 'Consul for Life'.
1803   Britain and France declare war again.
1804   Napoleon becomes 'Emperor'.
1805   Battles of Trafalgar and Austerlitz.
1806   Battles of Jena and Auerstadt.
1807   Treaty of Tilsit between France and Russia.

Moscow

None of Napoleon's brilliant victories would have been possible without the heroic, French, revolutionary armies, the first truly national armies in European history. One and a quarter million Frenchmen were called up between 1799 and 1805. (Although a quarter of these were judged unfit to fight because they were under five feet tall, the average height of Frenchmen at the time.) The regiments were a careful mixture of new recruits and battle-hardened veterans from the heady days of revolution, and the soldiers were highly motivated compared to soldiers from other countries. Discipline was kept without the extreme punishments used by most armies of the time. There was no cat-o-nine-tails as used by the British and no beating with the knout as in the Russian army.

In June 1812, a large part of this formidable fighting machine, 600,000 strong and stuffed with yet more new recruits, set off for Russia which was once again at war with France. Behind them they left a savage war for independence in Spain, backed by a British army under General Wellington.

For weeks, Napoleon's *Grande Armée* advanced across the vast, bleak Russian landscape and the Russians retreated before them, burning villages and removing all supplies of food. Smolensk was defended but then the Russians retreated again, towards Moscow. Finally, on 7 September 1812, they turned to fight. The spot chosen for the battle was near the small village of Borodino, 110 kilometres west of Moscow. Borodino was the most horrific of all the battles of the Napoleonic Wars. It was a French victory but at terrible cost - 58,000 Russian casualties to 30,000 French. Part of the reason for the death rate was that medical facilities on both sides were almost non-existent. To be wounded meant a high likelihood of death.

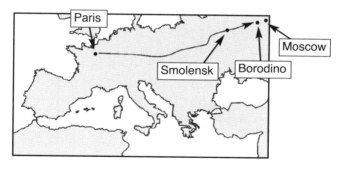

The *Grande Armée* entered Moscow a week later, on 14 September. Next day a fire was started accidentally by French soldiers lodging in one of the wooden mansions of the town and for five days the mainly wooden town burned like a bonfire. By the end, the city was uninhabitable. And now winter was about to set in. The French soldiers did not have adequate winter clothing because Napoleon had been gambling on a quick victory.

There was no choice left but to order an immediate retreat.

On 14 October, a day after the first winter snow began to fall, the huge army set off again, weighed down with loot but with very little in the way of food. In appalling, freezing-cold conditions and harassed by the Russians they started the long journey home. It was a journey into hell. Of the 600,000 who set out, only 90,000 made it back to France.

Island retreats

After Moscow, Napoleon was a changed man. He discovered a fondness for good food and slept more than he used to and he had difficulty concentrating. He still talked incessantly but now his main theme was how other people were to blame for the disaster of Moscow and not him.

In fact, despite his blustering, the war was already lost. Paris fell to the Russians and their Prussian and Austrian allies on 31 March 1813. On Easter Sunday 10 April, Tsar Alexander of Russia himself attended a solemn service in the Place de la Concorde, at the very spot where the guillotine had removed the heads of first Louis XVI and then the unfortunate Marie-Antoinette, his queen.

In April 1814, Napoleon was sent to the small Isle of Elba in the Mediterranean which, with remarkable generosity, the Allies allowed him to rule as a sort of mini-monarch. A week after he left, Louis XVIII*, younger brother of Louis XVI, was placed on the French throne by the victorious allies.

*Louis XVII (1785-95), second son of Louis XVI, had been king in name only, in prison on the execution of his father. Aged ten, he's reputed to have been poisoned while in captivity.

A few months of boredom and inactivity on Elba were too much for Napoleon. He paced the island, wrote hundreds of letters - and plotted. The following January, 1815, he returned to France. Once back on home turf, he quickly ousted Louis XVIII and ruled again for a further hundred, unhappy days - until 18 June 1815. On that day, at Waterloo in what is now Belgium, he was defeated finally and definitively by a British army under the Duke of Wellington and a Prussian army under Gebhard von Blücher.

The Battle of Waterloo brought to a close almost twenty-three years of war. This time the British and their allies were taking no chances. Napoleon was taken under guard to the tiny, remote, south-Atlantic island of Saint Helena. And there he stayed, a caged giant, until his death in 1821.

CITIZEN KING
AND THE JULY MONARCHY

In brief - the Nineteenth Century

Nineteenth-century France is confusing. The French kept changing their system of government:

1814/15-30	Return of the Bourbons - monarchy restored after the fall of Napoleon.
1830-48	*July Monarchy* - middle classes take over under Louis-Philippe, the Citizen King.
1848-51	*Second Republic*, a short interlude.
1851-71	*Second Empire* under Napoleon III (also called Louis Napoleon), Napoleon Bonaparte's nephew.
1871-1945	*Third Republic*.

Return of the Bourbons

Napoleon was finished. In 1815, the victorious allies put Louis XVIII, younger brother of Louis XVI, back on the throne. Louis XVIII sensibly tried to calm tensions in post-revolutionary France. His brother Charles X, who succeeded to the throne in 1824, wasn't so clever. Charles was a reactionary toad. He tried to turn the clock back to the bad old days of pre-Revolutionary France when nobles were nobles and everyone else knew their place. He was forced from power in a popular uprising backed by middle-class businessmen in July 1830.

The Bourbons had had a last chance and blown it.

The July Monarchy

Actually, the Bourbons hadn't blown it completely. The next ruler was Louis-Philippe, eldest son of the Duke of Orléans, who had been a somewhat distant cousin of Louis XVI and one of the most senior noblemen in France before the Revolution. Despite his noble status and the royal connection, the Duke of Orléans had made a name for himself as a political reformer in the National Assembly of 1789 and when the Bastille fell. In 1792 when noble titles were abolished, he became simply Philippe Egalité, Citizen. Sadly, he was executed in November 1793 at the height of the Terror.

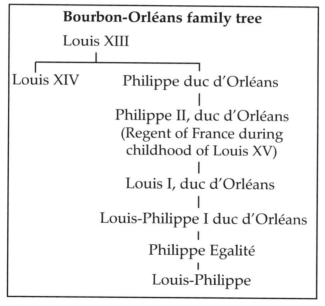

Bourbon-Orléans family tree

Louis XIII

Louis XIV — Philippe duc d'Orléans

Philippe II, duc d'Orléans
(Regent of France during
childhood of Louis XV)

Louis I, duc d'Orléans

Louis-Philippe I duc d'Orléans

Philippe Egalité

Louis-Philippe

Like his father but a lot cleverer, Louis-Philippe also flirted with radical politics. He joined the Jacobin Club in 1790 and then enlisted in the Revolutionary army and fought bravely. In 1793, at the same time as it was arresting his father, the Revolutionary Convention put a price on Louis-Philippe's head as well. He took refuge in

Switzerland and worked for a time as a schoolmaster before moving to America and then settling in Britain. Tales of his schoolmastering days were among his favourite after-dinner anecdotes in later life.

Louis-Philippe soon lost his early radical notions. He became a banker. As a minor Bourbon, he also became a natural focus for French opposition to the obnoxious Charles X in the late 1820s. In July 1830, when Charles X was pushed from power, Louis-Philippe crossed the Channel from his refuge in Britain and accepted the crown from his backers.

The 'July Monarchy', as Louis-Philippe's reign is called after the revolution which started it, was good for France despite its failings. Louis-Philippe was mainly interested in keeping the peace and making money. He liked to walk around Paris like an ordinary citizen. As he put it:

Je me moque absolument de l'etiquette ('I've no time at all for etiquette'.)

This was monarchy without the frills. The royal family lived like any other upper middle class family: loving, solid and respectable. One of Louis's friends once apologised for entering the royal presence *without* first muddying his boots. On holidays, the royal family would set off for the seaside in a charabanc (a horse-drawn coach).

1848
Despite solid achievements, including completion of Napoleon's Arc de Triomphe, the July Monarchy was

never secure. There were several attempts to assassinate Louis-Philippe. He was constantly hounded - by supporters of the ousted Bourbons on the right, by Bonapartistes who hankered for strong government in the middle and by radical socialists on the left.

But thanks to Louis-Philippe's efforts, industrialisation gathered pace in the 1830s and 1840s. Wealth increased - for the wealthy - but in the new mines and mills, workers worked long hours in dismal conditions for low wages. In their despair, many of them listened to a gospel of equality and socialism preached by revolutionaries such as Karl Marx, the founder of communism, in Paris in the mid-1840s.

Things came to a head on the night of 22/23 February 1848. In Paris the uprising began, appropriately enough, with a banquet. Fearing trouble, Louis-Philippe had banned all public political meetings, and, to get round this, leaders of the opposition organised a campaign of public 'banquets' throughout the country which was due to climax at a monster banquet in Paris set for 22 February. Louis-Philippe banned the banquet - and the revolution began.

That night of 22/23 February, barricades went up all over Paris and insurgents took to the streets in ever greater numbers. There was sporadic fighting with loyal troops attempting to keep order. By the morning of 24 February, a large crowd of insurgents was within two hundred metres of the Tuileries Palace where Louis-Philippe had set up home. Rather than spill more French blood, he chose to abdicate. He took refuge in England once more.

The Crown at Twickenham

That autumn (1848), the ex-royal family were getting used to another exile in Britain. While their new home on the outskirts of London was being replumbed, they moved into temporary accommodation at a pub called the Star and Garter in Richmond. Richmond was well known to Louis-Philippe because he'd lived happily for several years in neighbouring Twickenham during his first British exile forty years before. He'd even been known to frequent one or two of the local pubs. One day, he decided to revisit old haunts and took a walk into Twickenham. A stranger came up and greeted him warmly.

'Don't you remember me, Your Majesty?' said the stranger, shaking the King's hand. 'I used to keep The Crown.'

'That's more than I did,' said Louis, quick as a flash.

France has had several very decent kings. Henri IV was probably the best of them but Louis-Philippe is in the running.

If you're in London

The Crown Inn is still there, at 174 Richmond Road, Twickenham. Also in Twickenham, there's Highshot House on Crown Road where Louis-Philippe lived with his two younger brothers 1800-07, and Orléans House by the River Thames, where he lived 1815-17, which is now a gallery and open to the public

---

SECOND EMPIRE
AND ANOTHER NAPOLEON

But first - The Second Republic

Back in Paris, once Louis-Philippe was out of the way, the victorious revolutionaries proclaimed the 'Second Republic', and granted the vote to all male citizens, a very radical move at that date. However, this had the unfortunate result, as far as radicals were concerned, that they were outvoted by moderates in elections to a new Constituent Assembly shortly after. Among those elected was a middle-aged nephew of Napoleon Bonaparte called Louis Napoleon, recently returned from exile, who presented himself as a left-wing candidate and traded on his famous name to win popular support.

Thus by a twist of fate, it was a Bonaparte - Louis Napoleon - who became the first democratically elected President of France that December.

Louis Napoleon's background

1779   The future Empress Josephine marries Comte Alexandre de Beauharnais.

1783   Hortense, their second daughter, is born.

1794   Alexandre de Beauharnais goes to the guillotine during the Terror.

1796   Josephine remarries to Napoleon Bonaparte.

1802   Josephine's daughter Hortense marries Louis Bonaparte, brother of her step-father Napoleon.

1808   Louis Napoleon (the future Napoleon III), third child of Hortense and Louis Bonaparte, is born.

Napoleon III*

France might still be enjoying its Second Republic if it wasn't for Louis Napoleon. Exiled along with all the other Bonapartes back in 1815, when still a child, he grew up determined to restore the family's honour - and the family crown. In 1836, he tried to seize control of Strasbourg, then under French control, failed and was exiled to America. (With typical generosity, Louis-Philippe arranged for payment of Louis Napoleon's fare.) In 1840 he tried again, landing at Boulogne with a group of armed supporters. This time he was sentenced to

indefinite imprisonment. He escaped in 1846 and went into exile once again.

When first elected President in 1848, Louis Napoleon made liberal noises and was popular with the poorer sections of society. Meantime he moved quickly to gather the reins of power, placing trusted supporters in command of the army and in important ministries. His real agenda was to rule alone. In 1851 he moved sharply to the right and executed a coup against the very Republic of which he was President. Thousands of opponents were arrested and deported. But despite the

*Napoleon II (1811-32) was the only son of Napoleon I by the Austrian Empress Marie-Louise. He was brought up in Austria from 1815 after Napoleon I's fall. That same year, Bonapartist loyalists in Paris proclaimed him Napoleon II, but he was 'deposed' five days later.

coup, he was still popular. Next year he organised a referendum and was confirmed as 'Emperor Napoleon III' by an overwhelming majority of votes. 'The Second Empire' had begun.

All the above might lead one to think that Napoleon III was a ruthless dictator, but in reality he wasn't. Most of the deportees were allowed back soon enough. His government was authoritarian but moderate. Above all, the Second Empire was a time of confidence. It was *brash*. Typical of it are the boulevards pushed through the heart of medieval Paris on the Emperor's orders.

There were two reasons for the new boulevards: to beautify the city and to reduce the risk of riots. The boulevards had no cobblestones (so useful for throwing from barricades) and they allowed straight fields of fire for troops. Louis commissioned a workaholic by the name of Baron Haussman to do the work, first showing Haussman a map of Paris with the basic new layout sketched onto it. Haussman constructed a number of wooden towers at various points round the city. Using these he was able to make a very accurate survey since they were taller than the surrounding buildings. Then he started building. He took sixteen years to complete his gigantic task, and many beautiful old buildings were torn down in the process. (It's estimated that he transformed 60% of the buildings of Paris.) They were replaced by the grand boulevards and buildings that we see today, also new bridges, the Opéra, the layout of the Bois de Boulogne and a brand new water and sewage system.

Empress Eugénie
The year after becoming Emperor, Louis Napoleon married a beautiful girl of Spanish origin called Eugénie Montijo. Eugénie's late father, the Count of Montijo, had

been a liberal who had fought for Napoleon I. Given the connection, Eugénie and her mother were in Paris hoping to benefit from the new Napoleonic regime. As well as being stunningly beautiful, Eugénie spoke three languages fluently and was an amusing talker.

Happy as a bear with a pot of honey, forty-five-year-old Napoleon III moved his young(ish) wife into the Tuileries Palace. There the newly-weds proceeded to redecorate - extravagantly. The Second Empire was nothing if not showy and Napoleon III was determined that his court should be as showy as possible - and nothing like the homely court of Louis-Philippe. He demanded imperial etiquette, supposedly based on the court etiquette of Napoleon I. Men had to wear knee-breeches and women were expected to be sumptuously dressed. Eugénie did her bit for the showiness by putting on endless balls and other festivities. It was all a bit flash and not quite respectable compared to other monarchies.

If you're in Paris
The Palace of the Tuileries was begun by Catherine de Medici in 1564. It once stood alongside the Palace of the Louvres but it was destroyed by fire during a communistic uprising known as the Paris Commune in 1871. However the gardens, designed by André Lenôtre (1613-1700), who also designed the gardens at Versailles, are still there beside the Louvre Museum.

Butchery

Being a Bonaparte, Napoleon III felt that France should pull its weight in the world. Under his influence, French colonials in solar topees expanded their activities in South East Asia and West Africa, thereby introducing French civilisation and the delights of *haute cuisine* to regions previously deprived. He backed the Suez Canal project, headed by the Frenchman Ferdinand de Lesseps, a cousin of Empress Eugénie, and completed in 1869.

Military glory was part of the Bonaparte package. Napoleon III joined the Crimean War (1853-56) in alliance with Britain and Turkey against the Russians. This was a departure from tradition in that France and Britain were on the same side for once. For his next adventure he helped the Italians against the Austrians in Italy. Commanding the French army in person, he won the battles of Magenta (4 June 1859) and Solferino (24 June 1859). Solferino was sheer butchery - three hundred thousand men hacking, stabbing and shooting each other with canon, rifle and bayonet for over fifteen bloody hours in a benighted spot on the edge of the Lombardy Plain. It was because of this battle that the Swiss doctor, Henri Dunant, set up the Red Cross.

Napoleon III too was appalled by the carnage. After Solferino, he seems to have had a change of heart. He'd always been a liberal really. From now on, workers were allowed the right to form trades unions and the press was granted greater freedom.

Then war intruded once again.

Sedan

The Franco-Prussian War started over a squabble between France and Prussia as to who should be the next king of Spain. The French objected to a Prussian candidate for fear of being sandwiched between Prussian-backed rulers in the north and south. The Prussians backed down.

Which should have been the end of it. Unfortunately, the French foreign minister, the Duke of Gramont, was an idiot, described by the Prussian Prime Minister Otto von Bismarck as 'the stupidest man in Europe'. Gramont demanded, via his ambassador to Prussia, that the Prussians give an additional, humiliating guarantee not to change their minds. This the Prussian king Wilhelm I refused to do. Bismarck, cunning as a fox, seized the opportunity offered by this French insult and made sure the Prussian newspapers heard about it - war was what Bismarck wanted for his own devious reasons. To make matters worse, the French press then demanded an apology for the Prussian king's 'rudeness'. Both sides worked themselves up into lather of self-righteousness from which there could be no turning back.

War was declared on 19 July 1870. The French were super-confident at the beginning but Napoleon III himself was worried. Solferino had given him a horror of senseless slaughter. Hoping to avoid a tragedy but fearing the worst, he took command of the French armies in person despite being ill, incapable and in pain. Eugénie packed his medicines with her own hands before he set off for the front, his face pale and his legs shaking under him with the strain.

The war was an even worse disaster than Napoleon III had feared. By the end of August, one French army had fallen back on the fortress of Metz, the other, with the Emperor in tow if not actually in command, was trapped at the fortress of Sedan, near the Belgian frontier. The Germans attacked Sedan with overwhelming force on 1 September. Realising that the battle was lost, Napoleon III wandered about the battlefield looking for the fiercest action in a desperate attempt to get himself killed, hoping that his death would somehow stop the bloodshed. He himself signed the surrender document, addressing it to King Wilhelm of Prussia.

Sir, my brother,
Having been unable to die at the head of my troops, it only remains for me to put my sword in the hands of Your Majesty.
I am Your Majesty's good brother,
Napoleon

Two days later, Napoleon III was deposed. He spent the last three years of his life in England, which seems to have been where nineteenth-century French kings went on retirement.

If you're in the north

The *Château fort de Sedan* (stronghold of Sedan), perched on a promontory above the River Meuse, is probably the largest feudal fortress in Europe. Building began in 1424 and the walls were strengthened many times over the centuries. Each master builder added to the thickness of the walls without destroying previous layers, so it's a unique record of building techniques. For over two centuries it served as the palace of the princes of Sedan, but after 1642, when Sedan became part of France, it was converted to a garrison fort protecting the northern frontier. It now houses a military museum.

The Paris Commune

On 26 March 1871, following the Prussian victory in the Franco-Prussian War, municipal elections in Paris led to a revolutionary city government taking over. This very radical government is known as the 'Paris Commune'. Laws passed by the Commune harked back to the Revolutionary Constituent Assembly of 1793. The Republican Calendar was reinstated.

In May, troops of the national French government entered Paris to put down the Commune and Parisian revolutionaries rushed to the barricades to resist them. During 'La Semaine Sanglante', the Bloody Week, around 20,000 revolutionaries were killed, many of them shot in cold blood after surrendering. A further 38,000 were arrested and 7,000 were deported.

THEY BUILT A TOWER
LA BELLE EPOQUE

In brief - Impressionists and things	
1862	Monet, Renoir and friends meet.
1874	Monet and friends are first called 'Impressionists' by a critic.
1885	Baron de Coubertin starts the International Olympic Movement.
1895	Lumière brothers make the first ever movie.
1889	Eiffel Tower built.
1894-1906	Dreyfus Affair.

Dog bites boy

One summer's day in 1885, nine-year-old Joseph Meister was on his way to school in the small town of Meissengott in Alsace when he was set on by a rabid dog. The slavering hound pushed him to the ground and savaged him repeatedly until beaten off with an iron bar by a passing bricklayer. The dog was put down and, if things had taken their normal course, in time Joseph would have died too, of rabies. However, the local doctor, an intelligent man who kept up with the latest developments, suggested that Joseph be put on a train and taken to see the great scientist Louis Pasteur in Paris.

Since the boy had been so badly bitten, Pasteur decided to risk a new treament previously only tested on animals. He injected Joseph with extract from the spinal cord of a rabbit which had itself died of rabies. This helped Joseph's immune system to build up strength to beat off the disease. He made a complete recovery.

Vaccination wasn't new - the Turks had first used it centuries before. What was new was that Pasteur understood how it worked. He'd already developed treatments for chicken cholera and anthrax in sheep. Pasteur had been able to make these breakthroughs because, some years before, he had discovered that many diseases are caused by tiny, hostile micro-organisms, a discovery which was one of France's greatest contributions to modern science.

> **If you're near Besançon**
> In 1827, the Pasteur family moved to Arbois on the east side of Arc-en-Senans. Pasteur loved Arbois and returned frequently throughout his life. In 1874 he converted the old family house into comfortable rural retreat, complete with laboratory. It's been preserved as it was when he lived there and is open to visitors.The house where Louis Pasteur was born (1822), at Dole, about 20 kilometres west of Arc-en-Senans, has also been made into a museum.

The late nineteenth century was a golden age for French scientists. Apart from Pasteur, it produced Polish-born Marie Curie who discovered radium and polonium, Antoine Becquerel who discovered radioactivity, the Lumière brothers who invented the first successful cine camera and produced the first movie and many, many others.

Pasteur himself had started his researches in a very French sort of way, back in the 1850s when he investigated why wine and beer go 'off'. He'd discovered that fermentation is caused by the action of yeasts on the unfermented drink. It was this discovery of the large-scale effects of very tiny organisms which led to his later work on infectious micro-organisms.

> **If you're in Lyon**
> The Lumière brothers worked with their photographer father at his home, at what is now called *25 rue du Premier Film* (metro *Monplaisir Lumière*) when creating the first movie ever made *La Sortie des ouvriers de l'usine Lumière (Workers leaving the Lumière Factory)*. The family house is now the *Institut Lumière* and is well worth a visit.

A nasty bug

Pasteur's great book summarising his conclusions about fermentation, *Etudes sur le Vin* (Studies of the Vine), was printed in 1866. At that time the French wine industry, indeed the wine industry of Europe, was under threat from a very unpleasant six-legged, yellowish-green bug rather like a greenfly.

Phylloxera, to give the bug its Latin name, was a native of the east coast of North America and its food was the sap of vines. American vines were resistant to it so its numbers were limited in its native land, but not so the vines of Europe, where it first arrived around 1858. The glorious vineyards of France, Germany and Italy offered almost endless opportunities for *phylloxera* to sate its appetite so it grew fat and multiplied. Nothing could stop its spread. Growers tried spraying chemical poisons. They tried injecting insecticides into the ground because *phylloxera* liked to feast on the roots. By 1875 the French vineyards had been almost wiped out. Only by grafting remaining native vines onto American root stocks was the obnoxious pest finally defeated. No one now knows if the alien, American root stock affected the quality of the grapes or exactly how French wines produced *before* the disaster tasted, but the testimony of old wine buffs of the early twentieth century suggests that wine has never tasted quite so good since.

Impressionists

American vine root stocks were first imported in large numbers in the 1870s, so this means that the wine in the bottles in Pierre Renoir's famous picture *Luncheon of the Boating Party*, painted 1880-81, is probably wine from *post-phylloxera* grapes, a small imperfection in this portrait of a near-perfect world - surprisingly perfect, considering that Paris had suffered occupation by the Germans after the Franco-Prussian war, then the communistic revolt known as the 'Paris Commune' and the horrendous reprisals which followed it. Somehow despite all these tragedies the city continued to flourish. Parisian culture of the late nineteenth century seems to have been artistic, romantic, playful and civilised all at the same time.

The Impressionists got their name from a painting by Claude Monet, *Impression: Sunrise*, which he contributed to their first independent show of 1874 - independent, that is, of the *Salon* of the official French Academy. The young artists at the heart of the Impressionist Movement had no choice but to exhibit their paintings independently because the official Academy kept rejecting their work. Their swift, free style of painting was disapproved of.

Renoir, Monet and their friends were interested in reality,

but not photographic reality. They were out to capture the passing quality of light. They frequently painted out of doors, working fast with vivid colours to capture the moment before it was gone. The play of sun on water, scudding shadows of clouds, a sudden gesture: these were the sort of subtle, transitory things which intrigued them most.

In brief - Impressionist highlights	
1862	Pierre Renoir, Claude Monet, Alfred Sisley and Frédéric Bazille meet at the studio of Charles Gleyre for private painting lessons.
1863	Edouard Manet paints *Dejeuner sur l'Herbe (The Luncheon Party)*, impressing the four friends.
1864	They retire to the forest of Fontainebleau to paint outdoors.
Late 1860s	Renoir and Monet work closely together at La Grenouillère, a resort on the River Seine.
1872	Monet paints *Impression: Sunrise*.
1874	First independent exhibition. They are given the tag 'Impressionists'.
Mid-1880s	The Impressionist group starts to dissolve.

Iron and steam

To return to *Luncheon of the Boating Party*. It's a painting of a group of Renoir's friends on a day out from Paris. They're a mixed, democratic group. The girl on the left is Aline Chariot, a seamstress whom Renoir later married, and the man facing her is Gustave Chaillebatte, a wealthy patron. These people are very different socially to the aristocratic subjects of Watteau's *fêtes galantes*.

Luncheon of the Boating Party

Aline Chariot

The luncheon party takes place on the balcony of the Maison Fournaise at Chatou, a restaurant beside the River Seine where rowing boats could be hired. Once an exclusive resort of the wealthy, Chatou and other towns along the Seine became popular with all classes in the 1870s because of the railways. It was only ten minutes walk from Renoir's studio in central Paris to the station of St. Lazare and, from there, there were trains every half hour to Chatou. Anybody could get there.

If you're in Paris
The Maison Fournaise has been lovingly restored to how it was in Renoir's time. It's still a restaurant and you can still eat there. The food is excellent.

The number of kilometres of French railroads increased fourfold during the Second Empire and continued to increase during the Third Republic. Change in the leisure activities of Parisians was only one aspect of the massive impact of the railways on society. France was now the second largest industrial power after Britain and the French were at the forefront of design and technology. It was in Paris that Etienne Lenoir invented the first, practical internal combustion engine, patented 1860.

Etienne Lenoir (1822-1900)

Etienne Lenoir was born in Belgium. He moved to Paris early in his career and there made many inventions, including the first internal combustion engine, based on a converted steam engine (1860). It ran on compressed coal gas and air. In 1862 he drove his 'Hippomobile', powered by a version of this invention, eighteen kilometres from Paris to Joinville in (just) three hours. Over 1,400 Lenoir engines were built. They were very reliable but were mainly used for powering pumps and printing presses.

The Eiffel Tower

France's amazing achievements were celebrated in a number of international exhibitions. For the exhibition of 1889, held to commemorate the centenary of the Revolution of 1789, a competition was held to choose a design for the central feature. The winner was the engineer Gustave Eiffel. He proposed an immense tower made entirely of wrought iron to serve as a sort of gateway to the exhibition. Among the losing designs was a plan for a vast guillotine - rejected as in poor taste.

Eiffel was an expert in using metals for construction. He'd already designed the frame for the Statue of Liberty, a gift from France to the United States in 1885. Construction of his tower began in 1887. Over the next twenty-one months, around 18,000 pieces of preshaped metal were transported in horse-drawn carts from his workshops on the outskirts of town to the site near the banks of the Seine, where they were assembled. The project was completed under budget and on time, which in itself was a bit of a miracle. At 300 metres, it was the tallest construction in the world for the next forty years.

Storm clouds and sport

There was an element of competition to the industrial exhibitions of the nineteenth century. The very first International French Exhibition of 1855 was meant to outdo the British Great Exhibition of 1851. In fact, all over Europe a whiff of aggressive nationalism tainted the air. Fearful of competing *too* hard in Europe, the great European powers competed to expand their colonial empires elsewhere. Competition got worse as the century drew towards a close.

The Frenchman Baron Pierre de Coubertin believed that healthy sporting competition might reduce tensions as well as being good for sport. He also believed that it would toughen up young Frenchmen so as to avoid a repeat of the humiliation of Sedan in 1870. He held a conference of sports enthusiasts in Paris in 1885. The delegates were wined and dined as only the French can do it, they listened to a *Hymn to Apollo* by the composer Gabrielle Fauré, watched a giant firework display - and agreed to everything de Coubertin had in mind. At the end of the conference, they founded the International Olympic Movement.

But sport alone could not stem the rising tide of nationalism. In France, as in Germany, things were getting nasty. In a famous case in 1896, a Jewish officer, Captain Alfred Dreyfus, was arrested for spying and sent to Devil's Island, a prison colony in the Caribbean. There was no substance to the charges against him but he spent two years in a mosquito-ridden hell hole before he was cleared. His conviction was the result of vicious anti-Semitism - the right wing simply didn't like Jews being in the army.

Captain Dreyfus's supposed crime was passing military

information to the Germans. The Germans were still a major threat, as they had been ever since the Franco-Prussian War. By the end of the century they'd overtaken France as an industrial power. To counteract the German threat, France formed an alliance with Russia in 1894 and with Great Britain, the *Entente Cordiale*, in 1904. The Germans meanwhile, fearful for their own safety, formed alliances to counteract the French, British and Russian alliances. By 1914 Europe was a tangle of alliances, like so much diplomatic spaghetti: if any one country attacked another from the other side, all the others would be sucked in.

And then on 28 June 1914, a Serb nationalist by the name of Gavrilo Princip shot dead Archduke Franz Ferdinand, heir apparent to the Austrian throne, in a street in Sarejevo in Bosnia. The Austrians declared war on the Serbs. Germany, an ally of Austria, declared war on Russia, an ally of the Serbs, and then declared war on France, an ally of Russia. Germany then invaded neutral Belgium to get at France and, finally, France and Britain declared war on Germany.

World War I had started.

WAR!

THE NIGHTMARE YEARS

In Brief - the War Years

August 1914	World War I begins.
September 1914	Battle of the Marne begins.
February 1916	Battle of Verdun begins.
June 1916	Battle of the Somme begins.
November 1918	End of World War I.
1933	Adolf Hitler becomes Chancellor of Germany.
September 1939	Start of World War II.
June 1940	German forces enter Paris. Pétain surrenders and sets up government in Vichy.
August 1944	French Resistance fighters rise up against German forces in Paris.
August 1944	German forces in Paris surrender to the Free French.

Battle of the Marne

World War I began badly for France, very badly - 850,000 dead or wounded in the first four months. The French commanders were totally wrong-footed by the Germans. German armies attacked Belgium (August 1914) and swept through it into France. Within a few weeks they were north of Paris and the French government had to move to Bordeaux for safety. But then, along the River Marne on 6 September, the French and a small British army turned and fought, although they were outgunned and the situation looked desperate. The commander of the garrison of Paris sent reinforcements in taxi cabs to beef up the French forces. After a long, hard battle, involving upwards of two million men on both sides, the French and the British forced the Germans back.

After that the two sides settled down along battle lines which stretched from Switzerland to the North Sea and the ghastly slogging match of trench warfare began.

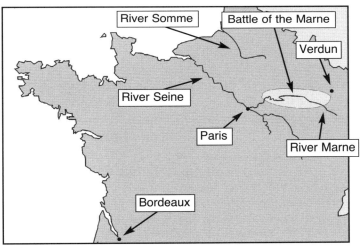

Verdun

The night of 22 February 1916 was a freezing nightmare for the men stationed in fortifications just to the north of the small town of Verdun in northern France. The Germans kept up a gas shell bombardment. Twenty-six-year-old Captain Charles de Gaulle, a future president of France, tried to keep up the spirits of his men but no-one got a wink of sleep. The hellish night was followed by a morning of conventional shelling, which stopped suddenly around 1 pm when a full German infantry attack started. The Germans quickly smashed through de Gaulle's sector. As de Gaulle and twelve of his men struggled through the mud in a desperate effort to regroup, a grenade was tossed from behind and de

Gaulle was stunned. He received a bayonet wound in the thigh and passed out. He spent the next two years as a prisoner of war.

De Gaulle was lucky to escape with his life. Verdun was the climactic French tragedy of World War I. As such, it can stand for all the other ghastly tragedies of those years. The Germans attacked Verdun with the deliberate intention of 'bleeding France white', of causing the maximum number of casualties - that and nothing else. The perverted reasoning of the German commander Erich von Falkenhayn held that, since there were more Germans than Frenchmen, the war could be won by a process of 'attrition' - when all the French were dead, there would still be a few Germans left over. As a result, 700,000 men from both sides died or were wounded.

If you're in Verdun
There are many monuments associated with the Battle of Verdun. Among the most moving is Douamont Ossuary containing the remains of 130,000 unknown French and Germans soldiers collected after the War. Another terrible monument is the *Tranchée des Baïonnettes* where an entire French regiment was buried and subsequently lost in its trenches during an appalling artillery barrage. The bodies were found three years later - hundreds of bayonets still thrusting through the soil.

General Henri Pétain

Conditions at Verdun were so extreme that the French continuously replaced the men at the front in a sort of conveyor belt process. During the eleven months of the battle, most of the French army fought there. It was known as the 'grinding machine'. The commander of the French forces at the most dangerous time was General

Henri Pétain, the son of a peasant family from north-west France. He became a popular hero both because he saved Verdun and because he looked after his men. Unlike Falkenhayn and many other generals, he didn't believe in squandering lives. He fought defensively because he understood that machine guns and other modern weapons gave the advantage to defenders: defenders, who were protected in trenches and other fortifications, could mow down attackers advancing over open ground. Attack was often little better than suicide. It was Pétain who recruited Captain de Gaulle into his infantry regiment back in 1913.

> **If you're west of Paris**
>
> From 1933 to 1970 when he died, Charles de Gaulle spent as much time as possible at his house at Colombey-les-Deux-Eglises, a pretty little town about 200 kilometres southwest of Paris. Although still owned by the family, the house is open to the public and you can see his office and library. There are guided tours (in French).
>
> While you're there, a short way to the south there's the Château de Cirey at Cirey-sur-Blaise, where Voltaire lived for fourteen years with Emilie de Breteuil. It has a perfectly preserved, early eighteenth-century theatre.

Peace and revenge

When the war ended on 11 November 1918, five years and 1,322,000 dead Frenchmen after it began, France was on its knees and the French prime minister Georges Clemenceau wanted revenge. At a peace conference held in Versailles the following year, France got back Alsace and Lorraine, lost after the Franco-Prussian War, and Germany was told to make huge annual payments in reparation for all the damage of the war.

The old world of boating trips on the Seine, lunch on long, sunny afternoons and dances in the open air, so familiar to Monet and Renoir, died in the trenches of World War I. Even the weather was worse in the 1920s than it was in 1914. All over Europe, people wanted to know why things had gone wrong and how to put them right. The weaker minded, or more idealistic if you prefer, fell for extreme solutions such as fascism and communism. In Germany, the Nazis went from strength to strength, fuelled by German bitterness over reparations payments. Adolf Hitler became Chancellor in 1933. Further east, Joseph Stalin, the Russian communist tyrant, crushed all opposition to his rule.

War again
Germany invaded Poland in September 1939, thus starting World War II. After a period of 'Phoney War' when nothing much happened, the Germans attacked westwards (April 1940) in a series of lightning *'Blitzkrieg'* attacks using tanks backed up by planes. They conquered Denmark, Norway, Holland and Belgium and then turned on France.

To avoid a repeat of the rapid German advances of World War I, the French had built a line of fortifications known as the 'Maginot Line' along the Franco-German border.

General Henri Pétain, hero of Verdun, with his preference for defensive warfare, had been a major backer of this project. The Germans simply drove round it, forcing some of the French forces and most of their British allies to escape to Britain via Dunkirk while the rest of the French forces fell back towards Paris or were surrounded and captured.

On 14 June 1940, the Germans entered Paris. Two days later, Henri Pétain, now eighty-four years old, was asked to form an emergency government in the defeated city. The doddery old man signed a humiliating peace agreement in the belief that he was saving France from total destruction. The Germans got Paris and most of France; Pétain's government got about a third of the country in the south. This rump state is known as 'Vichy France' because Pétain set up his government in the small, nineteenth-century resort of Vichy in the Auvergne. Vichy France lasted for two years, until 1942 when the Germans took control of the entire country.

Free French
Charles de Gaulle, who had risen to become a junior minister in the French government, was disgusted by Pétain's capitulation. He was in London on a government mission in June 1940 when the Germans entered Paris. From there he made a historic radio broadcast to the French people:

> *I, General de Gaulle, currently in London, invite the officers and French soldiers ... with their weapons or without their weapons... to put themselves in contact with me ...*

Next morning, his temporary London offices were besieged by French people offering their help.

France's long fight-back had started. Without a country and with no money worth speaking of, the Free French, as French troops not under German or Vichy control were called, were very weak but they were determined. De Gaulle put himself at their head. He broadcast regularly to those of his fellow countrymen living under German occupation, to the French Resistance and to those living in Vichy France - which was almost the same as being under German occupation. When the war was almost over and the British, American and Allied forces were advancing across France following the D-Day landings, de Gaulle's Free French forces entered liberated Paris in advance of the rest of the allied forces. They received the German surrender there.

After the war, Pétain was sentenced to death. The Vichy government had been far too willing to follow German orders, even to the rounding up of Jews for the Nazi gas chambers. Remembering former loyalties, de Gaulle had the sentence altered to life in solitary confinement. Pétain spent his final six years, until his death in 1951, imprisoned on the tiny Ile d'Yeu off the Brittany coast.

Pétain

When he died in July 1951, Pétain was ninety-five years old. His portait meanwhile had been taken down from the 'Room of Honour' beneath the citadel of Verdun and his name obliterated from a plaque listing freemen of the city. However, a burial plot has been reserved him outside the Douamont Ossuary. So far the French authorities have refused permission for his reburial there.

IS EUROPE BORING?
IT ALL DEPENDS

In Brief - since World War II	
1951	European Coal and Steel Community founded.
1954	French leave Indo-China.
1957	Treaty of Rome - Common Market founded
1958	Algerian revolt, start of the Fifth Republic.
1968	Worker/student riots in Paris.
1969	Charles de Gaulle retires.
1993	Maastricht Agreement for European Union approved.
2002	Euro replaces the franc as France's official currency.

Peace

There's been no war on French soil since 1945. After the carnage of the previous two hundred years that's almost a miracle.

The Third Republic expired in 1940 when the Germans entered Paris. The Fourth Republic which replaced it was born in 1946 from the ashes of war and after a short period of emergency rule by de Gaulle. It was always a shaky edifice. Fourth-Republic governments lasted six months on average. But the Fourth Republic for all its shakiness boasts one crowning achievement - it forged the European Union, or rather, what would become the European Union.

The idea of tying France and Germany by their wallets,

so to speak, first occurred to a politician called Jean Monnet from Cognac (where the brandy comes from). He proposed an economic link between France and West Germany to be called the 'European Coal and Steel Community'. It would embrace Italy, Holland, Belgium, Luxembourg, France and West Germany, making 'the Six' - France and West Germany being the ones which really mattered of course. West Germany had the iron, France had the coal to forge it. As Monnet pointed out, if the two countries were totally dependent on each other for steel production, war between them would be impossible because guns and tanks are made of steel and you can't make war without guns and tanks.

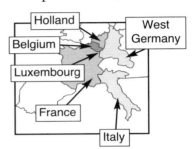

Monnet's idea was taken up by Robert Schuman, a leading politician in the Fourth Republic. Much negotiation in smoke-filled rooms gave birth to the European Coal and Steel Community in 1951. This led to the Treaty of Rome, signed in 1957, forming the EEC (European Economic Community), the EC (European Community, 1967) and finally to the European Union of today.

People tend to gripe about European union. They say that it's boring, which it is, that it's inefficient, which it is, that it's expensive, which it is, and that it isn't working properly - which it isn't. Where it *really* matters it works very well indeed.

It keeps the peace.

Being boring can be a virtue.

No more empires

De Gaulle never liked European union. *'Le Grand Charlie'* was a French patriot first, last and in between. But when he came back into power in 1958, he had to put up with Europe because it was so popular with the French people. They saw the point even if he didn't.

That year, things were going badly. In fact they were in crisis. The French overseas empire, so carefully built up by Napoleon III, was disintegrating. Vietnam in French Indo-China had gone already. Now brutal measures were being used to crush an independence struggle in Algeria in North Africa. Disgusted by the violence, the public voted in a new government to negotiate with the rebels. From the point of view of French Algerian colonists and their backers, the French Empire was in danger from this new government. Opponents of the new government took to the streets of Paris, backed by officers in the French army. These officers planned a military coup but fortunately the army rank and file refused to follow them.

Enter de Gaulle, great white hope of the army officers and the right wing. Surely de Gaulle wouldn't allow a chunk of the French Empire to break away without a fight - would he?

De Gaulle refused to have anything to do with a military coup. He stood aloof. When finally invited to form a government, he ruled by decree for six months and the most he did by way of a coup was to write a new constitution - for a *Fifth* Republic. He'd never liked the Fourth one. To add insult to injury as far as the right wing was concerned, the following year he announced 'home rule' for Algeria, expanded to full independence in 1962.

France still has the Fifth Republic. Apart from a little blip in 1968 when de Gaulle was called out of retirement one last time, it's still going strong. After nearly fifty years, that's not bad - for France.

But who cares anyway? As we've seen, this beautiful and creative country has a remarkable knack for keeping going regardless of all the constitutions, republics, empires, monarchies, revolutions and foreign occupations which it's had to suffer. Perhaps it's the climate, perhaps it's the language, perhaps it's the result of drinking white wine for breakfast while clad in a shabby vest (you know what I mean), perhaps it's sheer bloody-mindedness - whatever French culture is, it's stronger than any government.

Long may it continue. Without France, the world would be a very much poorer place. As they say (for the time being at least):

Vive la République!

THE RULERS OF FRANCE

Merovingians

During the Merovingian period the land of France was frequently divided, with several minor kings ruling simultaneously in different places. Included on this list for this period are the most important Merovingian kings, but not the minor ones.

Clovis I 482-511
Childerbert I 511-58
Clotaire I 558-62
Caribert 562-66
Chilperic I 566-84
Clotaire II 584-628
Dagobert I 628-37
Clovis II 637-55
Clotaire III 655-68
Childeric II 668-74
Thierry I (Theodoric I) 674-91
Clovis III 691-95
Childebert II 695-711
Dagobert III 711-16
Chilperic II 716-21
Thierry II 721-37

Carolingians
Pepin the Short 751-68
Charlemagne 768-814
Louis I, the Pious 814-40
Charles I, the Bald 840-77
Louis II, the Stammerer 877-79
Louis III 879-82
Carloman 882-84
Charles II, the Fat 844-88
Odo, Count of Paris 888-98

Charles III, the Simple 898-922 (died 929)
Robert I 922-23
Raoul 923-36
Louis IV, the Foreigner 936-54
Lothaire 954-86
Louis V, the Sluggard 986-989

Capetians
Hugh Capet 987-96
Robert II, the Pious 996-1031
Henri I 1031-60
Philip I 1060-1108
Louis VI, the Fat 1108-1137
Louis VII, the Young 1137-80
Philip II, Augustus 1180-1223
Louis VIII, the Lion 1223-26
Louis IX (Saint Louis) 1226-70
Philip III, the Bold 1270-85
Philip IV, the Fair 1285-1314
Louis X, the Quarreller 1314-16
Philip V, the Tall 1316-1322
Charles IV, the Fair 1322-28

Valois
Philip VI 1328-50
John II, the Good 1350-64
Charles V, the Wise 1364-80
Charles VI, the Well-Loved 1380-1422
Charles VII, the Victorious 1422-61
Louis XI, the Spider 1461-83
Charles VIII 1483-98
Louis XVII, Father of the People 1498-1515
Francis I 1515-47
Henri II 1547-59
Francis II 1559-60

Charles IX 1560-74
Henry III 1574-89

Bourbons
Henri IV of Navarre 1589-1610
Louis XIII 1610-43
Louis XIV, the Sun King 1643-1715
Louis XV, the Well-Beloved 1715-74
Louis XVI 1774-93

First Republic
National Convention 1792-95
Directory 1795–99

Consulate
Napoleon Bonaparte 1799-1804

First Empire
Napoleon I 1804-15

Restoration of the Bourbons
Louis XVIII, le Désiré 1814-24
Charles X 1824-30

July Monarchy
Louis-Philippe, 'Citizen King' 1830-48

Second Republic (President)
Louis Napoleon 1848-52

Second Empire
Napoleon III (Louis Napoleon) 1852-70

Third Republic (Presidents)
Louis Adolphe Thiers 1871-73

Marie de MacMahon 1873-79
François Grévy 1879-87
Sadi Carnot 1887-94
Jean Casmir-Périer 1894-95
François Félix Faure 1895-99
Émile Loubet 1899-1906
Clement Armand Fallières 1906-13
Raymond Poincaré 1913-20
Paul E. L. Deschanel 1920-20
Alexandre Millerand 1920-24
Gaston Doumergue 1924-31
Paul Doumer 1931-32
Albert Lebrun 1932-40

Vichy Government (Chief of State)
Henri Philippe Pétain 1940-44

Provisional Government (Presidents)
Charles de Gaulle 1944-46
Félix Gouin 1946-46
Georges Bidault 1946-47

Fourth Republic (Presidents)
Vincent Auriol 1947-54
René Coty 1954-59

Fifth Republic (Presidents)
Charles de Gaulle 1959-69
Georges Pompidou 1969-74
Valéry Giscard d'Estaing 1974-81
François Mitterrand 1981-95
Jacques Chirac 1995-

Important Dates

BC

c.90,000	Neanderthalers roam western Europe.
c.37,000	Cro-Magnons start to replace the Neanderthalers.
c.15,000	Cave paintings of Lascaux.
c.5,000-	Stone-building culture of Carnac.
c.1,200-	Celtic invasions.
c.600	Foundation of Marseille by the Greeks.
c.390	Celts burn Rome.
121	Formation of the Roman 'Province'.
52	Julius Caesar defeats the Gauls under Vercingetorix.

AD

c.258	Saint Denis martyred by the Romans.
275-76	Major invasion by German tribes driven off but Roman Empire starts to decline.
481	Start of first Frankish kingdom under Clovis.
496	Clovis baptised by the Catholic bishops.
732	Charles Martel defeats the Arabs outside Tours.
754	Pepin the Short anointed with holy oil by the Pope.
800	Charlemagne proclaimed Holy Roman Emperor by Pope Leo III.
911	Charles the Simple appoints Rollo Count of Rouen - the start of Normandy.
987	Hugh Capet, the first Capetian, becomes king.
1096	First Crusade.
c.1130	Start of Gothic architecture.
1337	Start of the Hundred Years' War.
1346	Battle of Crécy.
1348-9	Black Death.

1429	Joan of Arc captures Orléans.
1453	End of the Hundred Years' War.
1523	First Huguenot martyr burned in Paris.
1572	Saint Bartholomew's Day Massacre.
1589	Henry IV of Navarre becomes the first Bourbon king of France.
1598	Edict of Nantes grants religious toleration to Huguenots.
1614	Marie de Medici summons a meeting of the Estates General.
1624-42	Cardinal Richelieu is Chief Minister to Louis XIII.
1635	France joins the Thirty Years' War (1618-1648).
1642-61	Cardinal Mazarin is Chief Minister.
1643	Louis XIV becomes king.
1648-60	The Fronde rebellions against Mazarin and Louis XIV.
1661	Louis XIV takes over on the death of Mazarin.
1661	Work starts on the Palace of Versailles
1685	Revocation of the Edict of Nantes.
1701-13	War of the Spanish Succession.
1713-14	Treaties of Utrecht.
1751	The first volume of the *Encyclopédie*, the work of the *Philosophes,* published.
1756-63	Seven Years' War - France loses its colonies in India and Canada to Britain.
1788	Louis XVI summons the Estates General to meet at Versailles.
1789 June	Commons swear the Tennis Court Oath at Versailles.
1789 - July	Storming of the Bastille.
1789 - August	Declaration of the Rights of Man.
1789 - October	Women march on Versailles and take the royal family back to Paris.

1791	Royal family flees Paris but is captured at Varennes and taken back.
1792	Battle of Valmy. - the Revolution is victorious.
1793 - January	Execution of Louis XVI.
1793-94	The Reign of Terror.
1793 - October	Republican calendar introduced.
1794	Metric system adopted.
1794 - July	Execution of Robespierre.
1795-99	Rule by the Directory.
1799	Napoleon seizes power - the Consulate established.
1802	Treaty of Amiens - peace declared with Britain.
1803	USA buys Louisiana from France - the 'Louisiana Purchase'.
1804	Napoleon crowned Emperor.
1805 - August	French fleet defeated at the Battle of Trafalgar.
1805 - December	Battle of Austerlitz.
1806	Battles of Jena and Auerstadt.
1807	Treaty of Tilsit signed with Russia.
1812	Napoleon's invasion of Russia.
1814	Napoleon sent to island of Elba - Bourbon monarchy re-established under Louis XVIII.
1815 - January	Return of Napoleon - the 'One Hundred Days'.
1815 - June	Battle of Waterloo - Napoleon sent to the island of St. Helena.
1830 - July	Start of the July Monarchy under Louis-Philippe.
1848	July Monarchy overthrown - start of the Second Republic.
1851/2	Louis Napoleon establishes the Second Empire.

1852-65	Construction of the Paris boulevards by Baron Haussman.
1853-56	Crimean War.
1859	Battles of Solferino and Magenta.
1870-71	Franco-Prussian War.
1870 - September	Battle of Sedan.
1871	Paris Commune.
1871	Start of the Third Republic.
1874	Monet exhibits *Impression: Sunrise.*
1889	Centenary Exhibition of the Revolution - building of the Eiffel Tower.
1894-1906	Dreyfus Affair.
1914-18	World War I.
1914 - September	Battle of the Marne.
1916	Battles of Verdun and the Somme.
1939-45	World War II.
1940 - June	Start of German occupation - Vichy France established in the south.
1945	Start of the Fourth Republic.
1951	European Coal and Steel Community founded.
1954	France leaves Indo-China.
1957	Treaty of Rome - start of the Common Market.
1958	Algerian Revolt - start of the Fifth Republic.
1968	Student riots in Paris
1969	De Gaulle retires.
1993	Maastrict Agreement for European Union.

Index